≋ THE ≋
MYTHOLOGY OF
SUPERNATURAL

THE
MYTHOLOGY OF
SUPERNATURAL

THE SIGNS AND SYMBOLS BEHIND
THE POPULAR TV SHOW

Nathan Robert Brown

BERKLEY BOULEVARD BOOKS, NEW YORK

THE BERKLEY PUBLISHING GROUP
Published by the Penguin Group
Penguin Group (USA) Inc.
375 Hudson Street, New York, New York 10014, USA
Penguin Group (Canada), 90 Eglinton Avenue East, Suite 700, Toronto, Ontario M4P 2Y3, Canada
(a division of Pearson Penguin Canada Inc.)
Penguin Books Ltd., 80 Strand, London WC2R 0RL, England
Penguin Group Ireland, 25 St. Stephen's Green, Dublin 2, Ireland (a division of Penguin Books Ltd.)
Penguin Group (Australia), 250 Camberwell Road, Camberwell, Victoria 3124, Australia
(a division of Pearson Australia Group Pty. Ltd.)
Penguin Books India Pvt. Ltd., 11 Community Centre, Panchsheel Park, New Delhi—110 017, India
Penguin Group (NZ), 67 Apollo Drive, Rosedale, Auckland, 0632, New Zealand
(a division of Pearson New Zealand Ltd.)
Penguin Books (South Africa) (Pty.) Ltd., 24 Sturdee Avenue, Rosebank, Johannesburg 2196,
South Africa

Penguin Books Ltd., Registered Offices: 80 Strand, London WC2R 0RL, England

The publisher does not have any control over and does not assume any responsibility for author or third-party websites or their content.

This book is not authorized or endorsed by anyone associated with the *Supernatural* TV show.

PRINTING HISTORY
Berkley Boulevard trade paperback edition / August 2011

Library of Congress Cataloging-in-Publication Data

Brown, Nathan Robert.
The mythology of Supernatural : the signs and symbols behind the popular tv show / Nathan Robert Brown.—Berkley Boulevard trade paperback ed.
    p. cm.
Includes bibliographical references and index.
ISBN 978-0-425-24137-0
1. Supernatural (Television program : 2005–) 2. Horror television programs—History and criticism. I. Title.
PN1992.77.S84B68 2011
791.43'6164—dc22   2011014848

PRINTED IN THE UNITED STATES OF AMERICA

20 19 18 17 16 15 14 13 12 11

*This book is dedicated to the legendary
1967 Chevy Impala 327 V-8 four-barrel—the only car with
enough awesome to be driven into an Apocalypse
by Dean Winchester.*

ACKNOWLEDGMENTS

I would like to thank my editor, Danielle Stockley, for her work, guidance, and input on this project. I would also like to thank my new agent, Kim Lionetti, who is working hard to fill the big shoes left behind by her predecessor. I extend my most sincere thanks to everyone who was involved in the creation of this project.

CONTENTS

≈ THE ≈
MYTHOLOGY OF
SUPERNATURAL

INTRODUCTION

Ever since human beings took their first steps into the dark and frightening realms of existence, heroes have walked among us. And for just as long, human beings have loved heroes.

Perhaps we adore heroes because they are models for us. They display honor, loyalty, courage, and skill at levels we may never reach but strive for nonetheless—and we are better for it. Heroes represent the hope of every one of us: that, when it matters most, we will prove to be greater than we appear, braver than we feel, and stronger than we ever thought possible.

Perhaps we care about heroes because they are immortal, in a sense, in that even after death they are never forgotten. They live on within the hearts and minds of those who hear tell of their perilous journeys, violent battles, and courage in the face of almost certain defeat. Myths are meant to immortalize their heroic journeys.

For as long as there have been heroes, those half-brave, half-mad souls willing to dash headlong against things that would send most of us screaming in the other direction, there have been stories to immortalize their journeys. Through triumph and tragedy, through sin and salvation, through it all, we love them. And in the end, it doesn't matter whether or not any hero was ever, in the historical sense, truly alive. What really matters are the ways in which their myths affect those of us who are.

Sam and Dean Winchester are heroes—no doubt about that. Reality doesn't play into it. Who cares if they are real? They are real to the *Supernatural* fans who love them, and that is real enough. These fans have found a new set of brave, capable, headstrong, and often irreverent heroes to admire, each with their own unique set of strengths and weaknesses, virtues and flaws. Dean, Sam, John, Bobby, Ellen, and Jo, and even Castiel—we love them for all of it, the good along with the bad. This is what sets the heroes of *Supernatural* apart from cookie-cutter, run-of-the-mill TV tough guys—we love them for their flaws.

Being a mythologist by nature, I began the undertaking of this book with the preconceived idea that I was simply going to be identifying the mythologies and folklore used to create various monsters, events, and other elements of the *Supernatural* universe. And while I admit that much of the task of writing this book consisted of just that, something unexpected happened. As I watched more episodes of the show (and, I must admit, became an avid *Supernatural* fan in the process), I discovered that *Supernatural* isn't just a show that was developed by using mythology; it *is* mythology. The show is not just *based* on mythological figures and events; it is a new kind of myth, all its own.

The stories of *Supernatural*'s heroes are new manifestations of age-old myths, tales that have existed since the dawn of humankind. They are certainly not just carbon copies of old lore or mythical archetypes, however, but are unique in their own right. And the show encompasses the scope of mythology to such an incredibly broad degree that there are probably few traditional myths in existence that cannot be compared to some figure, event, relationship, or element of *Supernatural*.

Even the basic premise of the story, if summed up in general speech, sounds like it could come from the pages of some ancient epic:

> *Two young brothers, who are polar opposites in personality, lose their mother at the hands of a demon. They are raised as warriors by their father and, once of age, seek to take revenge on the demon that killed their mother. When their father dies, sacrificing his life and soul in order to save his oldest son, the brothers are guided by a wise, bearded mentor, a longtime friend and rival of their father.*
>
> *The path to vengeance, of course, never leads one straight to its destination. Before facing their nemesis the demon, the brothers face numerous setbacks and endure many difficult trials. Against terrible odds, they manage to clear every hurdle put in front of them until finally they have their chance. Using an enchanted weapon given to them by their father, they succeed in destroying the demon and avenging their mother's death.*
>
> *Vengeance, however, rarely (if ever) has a happy ending in such stories. There is an old proverb that warns, "When plotting*

revenge, you should dig two graves—one for your enemy, and the other for yourself." Often there is a price to pay for vengeance, the cost of which can be dire. The Winchesters may have killed the demon, but a gate to Hell is opened in the process and an army of new demons is unleashed upon the Earth. The land is flooded by evil spirits, and now the brothers must act in order to make amends for the horror they have set free.

Yet there are some things that can't be redeemed. As the brothers try to stop the demons, they unwittingly begin the end of times, and what began as vengeance becomes something far greater. The brothers must now face a demon far more powerful than the one that killed their mother. They must fight for more than vengeance, more than love or a sense of obligation. Long story short—they gotta save the world.

As with any mythology, there are going to be people who disagree with at least one interpretation or another, and I don't expect that this book will prove to be any different. I have done my best to create a book that explores the mythology of *Supernatural* as well as its mythos—the collective myths that make up a work or universe—in a way that is accurate, informative, and most of all interesting to read. Considering the broad and often hard-core scope of the *Supernatural* fandom, however, I am sure that there will be some who feel that this book does not do the show justice. In fact, this concern plagued me throughout the writing of this work. Yet I was often able to find some solace in the words of *Supernatural* prophet Chuck Shurley (aka Carver Edlund), which I think would make a fitting end to this introduction:

You try to tie up every loose end, but you never can. The fans are always gonna bitch. There are always gonna be holes. And since it's the ending, it's all supposed to add up to something. I'm telling you, they're a nagging pain in the ass.

—CHUCK, "SWAN SONG" (5-22)

≡ 1 ≡

THE WINCHESTER ARSENAL

I f one is going to dance with the devil, it helps to know the tune. In their war against the forces of evil, the Winchesters are far from unarmed. Choosing the right weapon for a particular supernatural foe is a crucial part of a hunter's everyday work. Interestingly enough, many of the weapons used by the Winchesters (salt, holy water, iron, and silver, for example) have very real origins in history, religion, and mythology. Furthermore, many of the detection tools, such as electromagnetic field (EMF) readers and infrared thermal scanners, employed by Sam and Dean to hunt down angry spirits are the very same instruments being used by today's real-life paranormal investigators.

The Winchester arsenal contains a unique weapon for just about every supernatural baddie one could conjure up. Covering the lore and origins for all of these tools in detail would take a book all its own. However, in this chapter you will learn about the mythology, lore, origins, and uses of some of the most commonly used hunter tools in *Supernatural*.

SALT: IT'LL KILL YA (OR AT LEAST IT'LL HURT LIKE HELL)

Well, then get the hell off my property before I pump you so full of rock salt you crap margaritas!
—BOBBY SINGER, "THE DEVIL YOU KNOW" (5-20)

These days, we use salt mainly for stuff like flavoring our food and melting ice during the winter. In the early days of human civilization, however, salt was thought to have magical properties. And this shouldn't be all that surprising when you think about it. After all, the salting of meats and vegetation made it possible for the earliest nonnomadic peoples to survive during the barren winter months when they could not grow food. Salt preserved the stored foodstuffs that would have otherwise turned rotten and putrid before they could be consumed.

Symbolically, various European cultures (such as the Celts) viewed the element of salt as associated with fertility and prosperity. During many ages of early human history, in fact, workers were paid their wages in salt (which is where we got the saying "A man worth his weight in salt"). As a result, salt also came to be associated with good fortune, which is why "spilling the salt" is considered a bad omen. This is where we get the old superstitious practice of tossing a pinch of spilled salt over one's left shoulder, which is meant to ward off bad luck.

Salt also has a religious significance, especially in the Judeo-Christian traditions. Canonical Hebrew texts mention salt in thirty-five different verses. When Lot abandons the doomed city of Sodom, knowing that the wrath of God is imminent, he is told that none in his family should look back as they flee (Genesis 19:17). Not heeding the warning, Lot's wife turns to glance over her shoulder and is immediately transformed into a pillar of salt. Though there is no way to validate it, there is a belief that associates this "look over the shoulder" of Lot's wife with the previously mentioned superstition of tossing salt over the shoulder to ward off bad luck. In the book of Judges (9:45), King Abimelech destroys the city of Shechem, and the verse explains that he had "sown salt upon it." Salt water can cause otherwise fertile farmland to turn barren. More than likely, this reference to salt was meant as a curse to prevent the ruins of the destroyed Shechem from being reinhabited.

The Christian messiah Jesus was also a big fan of salt. In his famous Sermon on the Mount, Jesus refers to those who follow him as the "salt of the earth." The apostle Paul of Tarsus once said in Colossians 4:6, "Let your voices be filled with grace, seasoned with salt."

Other traditions imbue salt with special properties, too. In the Hadith texts of the Muslim tradition, it is written that Muhammad once said, "Salt is the master of everyone's food. Four blessings were sent down from the sky from Allah: Fire, Water, Iron, and Salt."

Salt is also used as part of a number of Hindu Dharma religious ceremonies and festivals, and it is revered in Vedic/Hindu Dharma mythology as a divine element. For housewarmings, a mixture of salt and water is used to ward off any evil spirits that may try to enter the home. In the elaborate tradition of Hindu weddings, after the marriage ceremony and before the celebratory reception, the bride sits before each member of the groom's family one at a time. A bowl of salt is placed between the bride and the family member, who then places a coin into the bowl and simultaneously scoops up salt into his or her cupped hands. The bride and family member then take turns transferring the salt back and forth with cupped hands. This is repeated until all members of the groom's family have passed salt with the bride.

There are many other instances in which salt is used for religious or spiritual purposes. In the various Wiccan traditions (yes, there is more than one form of Wicca), for example, salt is seen as a purifying substance, often used to prepare an area for ceremonial use, and as a symbolic element of the Earth. Wiccans also use a salt-and-water mixture, sprinkled across the thresholds of doors and windows, to bar evil spirits.

In Shinto, the indigenous religion of Japan, salt is also used for purification rituals. Shinto priests and nuns use salt in the blessing of houses, meant to ward off evil spirits. A similar use of salt to bless an area, which has its roots in Shinto, can be viewed in the sport of Japanese sumo wrestling. During a before-bout ceremony, the enormous competitors first firmly stomp the ground once with both feet to frighten away evil spirits and then toss a handful of salt into the *dohyo* (wrestling ring) to purify the area.

In *Supernatural*, salt is portrayed as a pretty handy substance when it comes to barring demons and spirits. This is not a surprise since just about every mythological tradition claims that demons and evil spirits have an aversion to the stuff. Whether they are pouring it in front of a doorway or shooting it into a pissed-off ghost, the Winchester boys make it clear that no hunter "worth his weight in salt" should leave home without an ample supply of the stuff.

In the episode "Clap Your Hands If You Believe" (6-9), Sam Winchester found yet another use for salt while battling a rather nasty leprechaun. The writers integrated an old piece of lore that states certain fairy folk, when confronted with a spilled pile of salt or sugar, have an uncontrollable compulsion to count every single grain one by one.

GOOFER DUST

Goofer dust . . . Oh, you boys think you know somethin' about somethin' but not goofer dust?

—GEORGE, "CROSSROAD BLUES" (2-8)

Goofer dust is a powder used in voodoo, a religion brought to the Caribbean islands and southern United States by African slaves. The word *goofer* is believed to have derived from the Kikongo word *Kufwa*, meaning "to die."

While *Supernatural* portrays goofer dust as a substance that wards off demons, its traditional voodoo use is nothing of the sort. Goofer dust is a mixture of various ingredients, commonly believed to include things like white and/or black salt, sulfur, ashes, ground-up snakeskin (some sources say skin that is shed; others say you must actually skin a snake), powdered animal or human bones, iron shavings from a blacksmith's anvil, dried or ground-up manure, and graveyard dirt.

While Sam and Dean might not have touched the goofer dust George gave them if they'd known about the manure, it is actually the last ingredient, graveyard dirt, that seems to have the most influence on how the dust is used. Some sources say any dirt from a cemetery will do, but others claim it must be dirt from an actual burial plot. Either way, the idea is that spirit energy is taken from the dirt and mixed with the energy of the salt as a catalyst for all sorts of spells—love spells, good-luck spells (a favorite among gamblers), minor curses, or even spells meant to kill. The nature of the spell often requires dirt from a particular type of cemetery or grave site. For example, a love spell might require dust from the grave of a sibling, child, or close adult relative of the person casting the spell as these spirits would want the person to be happy and loved. Spells meant to cause injury, misfortune, illness, or death may require dirt from the grave of a person who died from illness, was murdered, or committed suicide, or dirt from a graveyard reserved for criminals. However, as with many magical practices, voodoo dictates that malevolent or harmful spells, which often require conjuring some pretty nasty spirits, may eventually backfire on the ones who cast them.

The one real-world voodoo use of goofer dust that most closely matches its portrayal in *Supernatural* is a basic spell of protection. In this case, the dust must include dirt from the grave of someone who loved the person to be protected. Another recipe for this protective dust offers broader protection, requiring the dust to be blessed by a voodoo priest and sprinkled with holy water. However, goofer dust is not normally used in voodoo to bar demons or spirits. This is probably because most voodoo spells involve contractual agreements with various spirit entities. A priest might tick off a spirit by barring it one day, and then be unable to invoke that same spirit later on when it is needed for a different type of spell. Voodoo is all about playing the politics of the spirit realm.

HEAVY METAL: IRON

About three thousand years ago, iron forever changed the face of human civilization. It replaced bronze as the primary metal used for making tools and weapons. Unlike the much softer bronze, iron was hard enough to easily chip most types of stone without taking any severe damage. Aside from being used for making tools and weapons, the element of iron has a long history of supernatural lore.

In European folklore, iron offers protection against fairies and other mythical creatures. Such lore claims that iron is especially dangerous to these creatures and that they can be harmed or even killed by merely touching the element. The powers of witches, for example, can be dispelled by tapping them on the forehead with an iron rod, while certain elements of werewolf lore (which, of course, did not make their way into the *Supernatural* mythos) claim that one can force a werewolf back into its human form by throwing an iron rod over its head. These sorts of stories may have resulted in the practice of enclosing cemeteries in wrought iron fences in order to keep evil or troublesome spirits from disturbing the restful dead.

SAM: What should we do?

DEAN: Fight the fairies! You fight those fairies! . . . FIGHT THE FAIRIES!

—SAM AND DEAN WINCHESTER, "CLAP YOUR HANDS IF YOU BELIEVE" (6-9)

In the episode "Clap Your Hands If You Believe" (6-9), the use of iron as a weapon against fairies is integrated into the mythos of the show. However, the writers took it a step further and integrated other forms of "sacred metals," such as silver. When the fairy folk came into contact with a number of different types of metal, it would burn their skin.

Some remnants of these beliefs about iron can still be found today. Ever heard the term *lucky horseshoe*? Believe it or not, the idea of lucky horseshoes gets its origins from a particular story from European Judeo-Christian folklore. This story, which dates from around 959 CE, tells of an encounter Saint Dunstan once had with the devil. Saint Dunstan, long before he became the archbishop of Canterbury, made his living as a blacksmith. One day, the devil came into Dunstan's shop and demanded that his horse be shoed. Seeing the devil for what he was, Dunstan grabbed an iron horseshoe and his tools, pinned the devil down, and nailed the horseshoe to the devil's cloven-hoofed foot. The devil cried out in pain, begging Dunstan to remove the shoe. Saint Dunstan refused to remove it unless the devil agreed that he would never enter any home or structure that had a horseshoe hung over its door. The devil begrudgingly agreed, and Dunstan removed the shoe and put the Prince of Evil out on his butt. This story is the reason why, to this day, you see a horseshoe hanging over the door of many houses in Europe.

Based on its universal portrayals in lore, it would seem that most spirits and demons have a natural aversion to iron. The use of iron on *Supernatural* is no different. By striking a spirit or ghost with an iron object, a hunter can temporarily dispel its form. While this is rarely a permanent measure, it's a good way to buy some time while the hunters try to find the spirit's physical remains to "fry up extra crispy."

The use of iron has even been incorporated in modern theories about the paranormal. The premise of how it works, however, has been updated. As will be discussed in further detail later in this chapter, spirit entities are believed to use electromagnetic energy in order to assume their forms (causing spikes on an EMF reader). Iron is said to act as a conductor, "grounding" the spirit's electromagnetic energy. When touched by iron, the spirit's electromagnetic energy would be drained or dispersed. The spirit is then forced to manifest its form all over again.

HOLY WATER

DEAN: What is this, holy water?
BOBBY: That one is . . . this is whiskey.
—DEAN WINCHESTER AND BOBBY SINGER, "DEVIL'S TRAP" (1-22)

Water is important. You would be hard-pressed to find anyone who would disagree with this statement. Sixty percent of the human body is made up of water. Our brains are 70 percent water. If you were to remove water from the Earth for just three days, nearly the entire human race would be wiped out, along with much of the planet's wildlife. The general rule of human survival states that only an already well-hydrated person can survive beyond three days without water. Even those previously well-hydrated few who managed to survive the three days would then suffer from extreme dehydration and need immediate medical attention. As important as it may be, for the hunters of *Supernatural* sometimes water alone isn't enough to get the job done.

In biblical writings, holy water is mentioned in Numbers 5:17, as God instructs Moses in how to perform a ritual meant to cure a "curse of jealousy," which roughly means that the ritual was supposed to prove the fidelity of any woman who had been charged with adultery by her husband. "And he shall take holy water in an earthen vessel, and he shall cast into it some of the earth from the pavement [or floor] of the Tabernacle." After the ritual, the woman would drink the holy water and earth mixture. If she was wrongly accused, then nothing bad would happen to her. If she was guilty, however, the holy water would turn to a curse that "will cause her belly to swell, her thighs [meaning her genitalia] to rot." You have to admit, this portrayal of holy water as a "bitter curse" is a far cry from how the substance is viewed in modern Christianity.

In the ancient Judaic tradition, a precursory ritual can be found that was similar to the later practice of baptism in Christianity. The ancient Israelites underwent a ceremonial purification, called *mikvah*, before entering the temple. The adherent would be immersed in "holy water" in a special ceremonial vessel. In modern Judaism, there is still a very similar practice of ritual bathing, called *mikva'ot*, the performance of which is usually reserved for special occasions such as weddings, during the Jewish holiday of Yom Kippur, or, especially among Israeli Jews, prior to entering the temple.

The Christian practice of baptism has its origins in the biblical New Testament, when Jesus went to see John the Baptist to receive this symbolic purification rite. Accounts of this event, which is believed to have occurred somewhere on the banks of the Jordan River, can be found in three of the four Gospels, those of Matthew, Mark, and Luke.

While the water that is commonly used in Christian baptismal rites or ritual bathing is certainly seen as "pure," it is not actually "holy water" in the traditional sense. So, how does one get holy water? To prepare water for sanctification, perform the following three steps:

Step 1: Get some water. Easy so far, right?

Step 2: Find a clean vessel in which to store the water while it is being blessed. A well-washed glass or metal bowl will do just fine.

Step 3: This step is sort of optional. If one wishes, a few pinches of salt may be added to the water. However, the salt must be "exorcised" before it is added (for more on the rite of exorcism, see chapter 7). Again, exorcised salt is not (according to most traditions) a requirement for making holy water.

Now it is time to actually bless the water, which may be done by reciting the following Latin blessing:

Deus, qui ad salute humani generis maxima quæque sacramenta in aquarum substantia condidisti: adesto propitus invocaionibus nostris, et element huic, multimodis purificationibus preparato, virtutem tuæ benedictionis infunde; ut creatura tua, mysteriis tuis serviens, ad abigendos dæmones morbosque pellendos divinæ gratiæ sumat effectum; ut quidquid in domibus vel in locis fidelium hæc unda resperserit careat omni immunditia, liberetur a noxa. Non illic resideat spiritus pestilens, non aura corrumpens: discedant omnes insidiæ latentis inimici; et si quid est quod aut incolumitati habitantium invidet aut quieti, aspersione hujus aquæ effugiat: ut salubritas, per invocationem sancti tui nominis expetita, ab omnibus sit impugnationibus defensa. In Nomine Domini Nostri Jesu Christi filium tuum, qui tecum vivit et regnat in unitate Spiritus Sancti, Deus, per omnia saecula saeculorum. Amen.

Roughly translated into English, the blessing goes as follows:

God, for Whom the salvation of the human race has built your greatest mysteries upon this established substance, in your kindness hear our prayers and pour down into this element the power of your blessing, prepared by many purifications. May this, your creation, become a vessel for Your divine grace to dispel demons and sicknesses, so that everything on which it is sprinkled, in the homes and buildings of the faithful, will be removed of all unclean and harmful things. Let no pestilent spirit, no corrupting atmosphere, remain in those places: may all the schemes of the hidden enemy be dispelled. Let whatever might trouble the safety and peace of those who live in these places be put to flight by this water, so that health, gotten by calling Your Holy Name, may be made secure against all attacks. Through the name of our Lord Jesus Christ, Your Son, Who lives and reigns with You in the unity of the Holy Ghost, one God, and forever, world without end. Amen.

While most Catholic priests tend to stick to the traditional Latin, there are no rules that specifically state that the blessing of holy water cannot be recited in English. Besides, there's more than one way to make water holy:

- **Saint or Nonliturgical Holy Water:** Often considered just as potent as traditional holy water (in some cases, more so), this form of holy water is found in "holy wells" or other water sources associated with Catholic saints. For example, there is one such place at a spring in Lourdes, France, from which Saint Bernadette Soubirous was told to drink during her eighteen visions of the Virgin Mary from January to July in 1858. Some make pilgrimages to this place in order to find healing.

- **Gregorian Holy Water:** This is traditional holy water that has been mixed with wine, salt, and ashes. It is commonly used for the consecration of religious sites, such as altars or churches.

- **Relic or Sanctified Holy Water:** This is water that has been "sanctified" by immersing a holy relic or religious object into it (or, depending on the relic or object, just touching the surface of the water can be enough). For example, an object such as a blessed rosary, Saint Benedict coin, or one of the many True Cross relic pieces would probably be enough to do the trick. Taking into account how often holy water has been used in *Supernatural*, one would assume that this is the Winchesters' preferred method for making it "on the fly."

Holy water, of course, is only useful against demons. When angelic forces descend upon the Winchesters, they need something with a little more kick. In the *Supernatural* mythos, there is only one way to contain the awesome power of an angel (aside from killing it with an angel sword or sending it back to Heaven with a banishing sigil, of course): holy oil.

HOLY OIL

DEAN: Where have you been?
CASTIEL: Jerusalem.
DEAN: Oh? How was it?
CASTIEL: Arid.

—CASTIEL, "FREE TO BE YOU AND ME" (5-3)

Needless to say, trapping an angel is not easily accomplished. Castiel has to travel all the way to Jerusalem (of course, for him it's a pretty short trip) to acquire a special oil that, when burned, will kill any angel who steps across it.

Where exactly did Castiel get the oil that was used to trap Raphael? There are two possibilities. In the ancient holy temple of

Jerusalem, fires were constantly burned in the seven intercon-
nected lamps of a holy menorah. These days, a menorah is usually
just a seven-branched candlestick. As it is written in Exodus 27:20,
God told Moses to "command the Israelites to bring you clear oil of
pressed olives for the light so that the lamps may be kept burning."

Then again, the oil used in *Supernatural* to make "holy fire"
may not be lamp oil. It could be another type of oil, called oil of
anointing. *Anointing* refers to the smearing of oil, usually on a person's forehead, as a symbol of divine right and/or influence. In a
later passage God gives instructions for the creation of this special
holy oil:

> *Take the following fine spices: 500 shekels of liquid myrrh, half*
> *as much of fragrant cinnamon, 250 shekels of fragrant cane, 500*
> *shekels of cassia—all according to the sanctuary shekel—and a*
> *hin* [1.5 gallons] *of olive oil. Make these into a sacred anointing*
> *oil, a fragrant blend, the work of a perfumer. It will be the sa-*
> *cred anointing oil.*
>
> —EXODUS 30:23–25

Holy oil remains in use in many of today's Judeo-Christian
traditions. For example, many evangelical and Protestant Christians use holy oil in exorcisms and blessings meant to ward off evil
spiritual forces.

We've talked about holy water and holy oil. However, these
aren't the only holy substances used as weapons against beings of
the spiritual realm. There is one more: the holy wood known as
Palo Santo.

PALO SANTO

ISAAC: Honey? Where's the Palo Santo?
TAMARA: Well, where did you leave it?
ISAAC: I don't know. That's why I'm asking.
—ISAAC AND TAMARA, "THE MAGNIFICENT SEVEN" (3-1)

Palo Santo can refer to a number of different species of tree, such as lignum vitae (also known as iron wood or wood of life), *Bulnesia sarmientoi*, or *Bursera graveolens*. Though its use requires no actual form of blessing or sanctification, the term *Palo Santo* is Spanish for "holy wood" or, as it is sometimes translated, "sacred wood," "saint wood," or "sanctified wood." It has long been revered in regions of South America for medicinal and healing purposes, as well as for incense making and even as a repellant for rodents.

It's holy wood, from Peru. It's toxic to demons, like holy water. Keeps the bastards nailed down while you're exorcising them.
—TAMARA, "THE MAGNIFICENT SEVEN" (3-1)

When essence from this wood is externally applied to the body, it can be used to treat a number of rashes and other skin conditions. Its bark and leaves can also be mixed with tea leaves to make a medicinal infusion that can treat certain stomach ailments.

In the folklore of certain regions in Ecuador, it is said that Palo Santo can be used to ward off various forms of *mala energia* (bad or evil energy).

Oddly enough, there is absolutely nothing in the lore surrounding Palo Santo that claims it can be used to "stake down" demons. The Palo Santo stake used by the husband-wife hunter team of Isaac and Tamara is likely no more than a creative reinvention of the writers for use in the mythos of the *Supernatural* universe.

A Palo Santo stake would have been almost as handy for fighting demons as Ruby's knife, and not nearly as hard to come by, so it's surprising that Sam and Dean haven't tried to get their hands on more of the stuff. Of course, sometimes a hunter has to stake down something that's a little more dangerous than demons, such as gods. When a rogue god just has to be ganked, forget the Palo Santo and reach for the "piney-fresh goodness" of an evergreen stake.

"GOT WOOD?": EVERGREEN STAKES

SAM: So what about Bobby? He's sure evergreen stakes will kill this thing, right?
DEAN: Yeah, he's sure.
—SAM AND DEAN, "A VERY SUPERNATURAL CHRISTMAS" (3-8)

As far as the mythology of evergreen stakes goes, there is a general belief that they should never be used to stake vampires. This stems from the belief in folklore that evergreen wood possesses properties of immortality. The idea is that an immortal being staked with an immortal wood would not be harmed and might actually be made stronger by it. When it comes to using evergreen stakes as weapons to kill rogue gods (even if they are disguised as a suburbanite elderly couple), as Sam and Dean have done on several occasions, there is little to no info available. However, it does reverse the above-mentioned idea and would seem to suggest that evergreen wood's immortal properties make it effective in slaying such immortal beings as the "old gods" of *Supernatural*.

THE COLT: A HISTORY OF ENCHANTED WEAPONRY

> Back in 1835, when Halley's Comet was overhead, same night those men died at the Alamo, they say Samuel Colt made a gun . . . a special gun. He made it for a hunter—a man like us, only on horseback. Story goes, he made thirteen bullets. This hunter used the gun a half dozen times before he disappeared, the gun along with him.
>
> They say . . . they say this gun can kill anything.
>
> —JOHN WINCHESTER, "DEAD MAN'S BLOOD" (1-20)

Perhaps no weapon in the Winchester arsenal is more powerful than the Colt, a legendary revolver made by Samuel Colt when Halley's Comet passed overhead on the final night of the Battle of the Alamo that, along with thirteen special bullets, is said to be capable of killing *anything*, whether physical or supernatural. The pistol used on the show is actually an impressively accurate replication of one of the first guns designed by the legendary American gun maker Samuel Colt—the 1836 Texas Paterson Colt. Considering that the lore of *Supernatural* claims Colt made the gun in 1835, a year prior, only adds to the mystery surrounding this weapon.

Shortly after the real Samuel Colt finished a lecture tour (though his lectures were really more like one-man shows, in which he dazzled audiences with unusual electrical contraptions), he used the money he'd saved from his road show as capital to secure patents and the means for manufacturing his single-barrel revolving pistol design, which he originally dubbed the Paterson Colt. At first he commissioned multiple well-skilled gunsmiths to fashion prototypes based on his designs.

You're saying your nukes are loose?
—DEAN WINCHESTER, "THE THIRD MAN" (6-3)

While the real Samuel Colt may not have made a revolver that could "kill anything," there is a long-standing mythical tradition about enchanted or blessed weaponry being used to destroy supernatural creatures. One such story actually comes from the annals of history and involves the bullet used to kill a monstrous wolf called the Beast of Gévaudan.

Beginning in June 1764, the surrounding area of the French region Gévaudan was being terrorized by an enormous animal. Initially the beast primarily attacked and devoured small children. For years more and more children continued to disappear, their shredded clothes and body parts often turning up later. Soon the creature upgraded to attacking small adults, usually women.

It was initially believed that the killings were just the work of a troublesome or rabid wolf. After a year of carnage, however,

King Louis XIV sent a unit of fifty-seven French Dragoons, specially trained soldiers once commonly used to spearhead military campaigns, to destroy the murderous animal. This part of the history also comes with a funny side note. After hearing of how the beast had attacked women, the commanding officer of the unit, Captain Duhamel, ordered a certain number of his soldiers to dress in women's clothing in the hopes that this would lure out the beast (special forces soldiers dressed in drag . . . talk about a weird mental image).

For months, the soldiers had a number of brief encounters with the beast. On a number of occasions, it was visually verified and/or reported that the wolf had been shot. However, the darn thing just wouldn't seem to die. At one point, convinced that his men had successfully killed the beast, Duhamel went back to France and received a hero's welcome. The celebration was brief, however, because a few days later a new report reached the capital. The beast was killing again. Duhamel was humiliated.

A number of famous French wolf hunters, such as the d'Enneval family and their close friend Antoine de Beauterne, were eventually called in to hunt down and destroy the beast. Time and time again, they were reported to have nailed the beast with direct hits. Beauterne even killed a giant wolf that measured in at six feet long from snout to tail, making it larger than most men of the period. Everyone breathed a brief sigh of relief. However, once again the killings resumed shortly after.

By this point, a majority of the Gévaudan locals were convinced that this ravenous beast was not a wolf at all. Some villagers began to claim it was a demon, or even the devil himself, taking the form of a wolf to torment them. Others believed it was a loup-garou, or werewolf. Regardless of what the people thought the creature was, just about everyone agreed on at least one thing by this point—if the military and the best wolf hunters in all of France could not destroy the beast, it meant that only God could save them now.

SUPERNATURAL FACTS

In the episode "Metamorphosis" (4-4), Sam and Dean encounter a cannibalistic creature called a *rougarou*. This term is a southern Creole transliteration of the French word for "werewolf," loup-garou. However, the French root was often used in ages past to refer to monstrous humans, such as murderers, rapists, serial killers, and (yes) cannibals.

Many of the residents of Gévaudan began making pilgrimages to the holy site of Notre Dame, hoping to invoke divine intervention. One of these pilgrims was a local hermit by the name of Jean Chastel. In an amazing show of foresight, Chastel took with him to Notre Dame a hunting rifle and three bullets. According more to legend than history, Chastel had these items blessed by the priests of Notre Dame.

Antoine de Beauterne returned to Gévaudan, hoping to redeem himself by finishing off the beast once and for all. He recruited every hunter who was willing to follow him, and his hunting party swelled to roughly three hundred men. Among these hunters was (you guessed it) Jean Chastel. The hermit carried with him the hunting rifle and three bullets he'd had blessed at Notre Dame. The enormous hunting party began combing the surrounding forests relentlessly for several days.

On the evening of June 19, 1767, the beast finally showed itself. The enormous creature, all fangs and claws, charged headlong at a group of hunters. This group included Jean Chastel, who immediately took aim at the beast with his blessed rifle and bullets. He pulled the trigger and nailed the creature with a direct hit. The seemingly unkillable Beast of Gévaudan went down—and this time it stayed down.

The killings ended for good. The beast's belly was cut open, and in its stomach they found freshly eaten human remains. Perhaps the beast was demon possessed after all. Apparently the people of Gévaudan just needed a blessed firearm. And as in *Supernatural*, a demon cannot be killed with just any firearm—they needed a specially enchanted and/or blessed piece of "boom stick" in order to get the job done.

Of course, you can't hit what you can't see. And when it comes to hunting ghosts, this can be a real problem. Thank goodness the Winchesters have their trusty EMF readers, allowing them to know when spirits are lurking close.

EMF READERS

SAM: Yeah, I know what an EMF reader is . . . but why does that one look like a busted-up Walkman?

DEAN: 'Cause that's what I made it out of . . . it's homemade.

SAM: Yeah, I can see that.

—SAM AND DEAN WINCHESTER, "PHANTOM TRAVELER" (1-4)

EMF stands for "electromagnetic field," and an EMF detector is a device that detects and measures the strength of electromagnetic energy in an immediate area. These devices were not originally designed for use in paranormal investigation but instead for electronics designers and others who need to detect electromagnetic radiation.

Over the last couple of decades the use of EMF readers among paranormal researchers has been steadily increasing. These devices work on the same principle as iron, in that spirits and demons manifest by using electromagnetic energy. Because of this, the presence of spirit entities will cause a spike in the electromagnetic field of the immediate area. Using an EMF reader allows one to detect such presences, as well as measure how powerful or close they might be by looking at how far the needle moves.

> **Am I haunted? . . . Am I HAUNTED?**
> —DEAN WINCHESTER, "YELLOW FEVER" (4-6)

No device is perfect, of course. And there are flaws in the use of EMF readers when it comes to gathering evidence in paranormal investigation. This is mainly due to the fact that spirit entities aren't the only things that can cause a spike in EMF. The truth is, just about any form of modern technology can cause this—cell phones, nearby power lines, even someone using a microwave in the same building. All of these can cause EMF readers to show a spike. The main problem is that researchers have yet to come up with a solid way to differentiate between EMF spikes caused by spirit energy and those resulting from normal, rational causes.

Then again, who needs EMF when you have a demon-killing knife?

LEMEGETON: THE *LESSER KEY OF SOLOMON*

SAM: And these protective circles . . . they really work?
BOBBY: Hell, yeah. You get a demon in one, they're trapped . . . powerless. It's like a satanic roach motel.
—SAM WINCHESTER AND BOBBY SINGER, "DEVIL'S TRAP" (1-22)

The *Lesser Key of Solomon*, or *Lemegeton*, has a lot in common with its parent text, the *Key of Solomon*. Despite the fact that this text directly claims authentic authorship from Solomon himself, it is unlikely that any of it contains his actual writings. As with the *Key of Solomon*, there are a number of different manuscripts that have claimed to be the *Lemegeton* over the years. The known manuscripts are, like the original, believed to be incomplete copies or imitations of information gleaned from Kabala adherents or Arabic mystics. However, unlike the *Greater Key of Solomon* (an alternative title for the *Key of Solomon*), this text deals almost exclusively with summoning demons and spirits.

The *Lemegeton* is divided into five sections:

1. *Ars Goetia*

2. *Ars Theurgia Goetia*

3. *Ars Paulina*

4. *Ars Almadel*

5. *Ars Notoria*

Within these five sections are instructions for detailed rituals and symbols, used for the conjuration of seventy-two specific demons and spirits. The names, roles, and uses for each of these demons and spirits are also explained in great detail. The truth is that most of the writings in this *grimoire* (which means, more or less, a book of spells or magic) are considered to be sensationalist portrayals of the real mystical practices that influenced them. This doesn't mean that some accurate information did not make its way into the text. You never know. But you probably want to think twice before you go messing around with the thing.

"THE KNIFE" AND THE
KEY OF SOLOMON

One specific section from book 2 of the *Key of Solomon* is titled "Of Sword, Knife, Pen, Lance, Wand, Staff, and Other Instruments." This section explains the markings and rituals for creating tools meant for use in magical rites.

In *Supernatural*, Ruby first introduces Sam and Dean to a dagger that can kill demons in "The Magnificent Seven" (3-1). This weapon is commonly referred to on the show as simply "the knife." However, the inscriptions on this special blade resemble those of Assyrian quadratic script. This script, made up of four-cornered letters, each uniquely divided into "quarters," likely originated in ancient Assyria. This same form of writing is shown in the *Key of Solomon*, in illustrations of knives and swords with magical inscriptions.

One of these tools is "the Knife with the white hilt." Most of the texts portray this knife as having a handle shaped as though made from polished bone or antler, just like the knife of *Supernatural*. The *Key of Solomon* illustrations also portray the upper-back edge of this tool's blade as having a forward curve almost identical to that of the blade on Ruby's knife. The biggest visual difference between the two is that Ruby's knife has a set of widely serrated teeth on the front edge of the blade whereas the blade illustrated in the *Key of Solomon* does not.

On a side note, among the instruments discussed in this section of the *Key of Solomon* text is "the Sickle." Interestingly, its shape strongly resembles the sickle belonging to the Horseman Death (for more on the Four Horsemen, see chapter 11). This same sickle was used by Alastair in his attempt to kill two reapers in "Death Takes a Holiday" (4-15) and later came into the possession of Sam and Dean before finally finding its way back to its rightful owner.

Of course, sometimes even the best hunter finds himself caught with his pants down. When there is no salt to be had, the holy water runs dry, and you lose your best demon-killing knife to a sadistic white-eyed demon from Hell, it is always good to have a fallback. More and more, Sam and Dean (and, of course, Bobby Singer) have become familiar with some pretty handy symbols and words that stem from a magical tradition known as Enochian magic (for more on Enochian, see chapter 2).

MOJO BAGS

Give me that mojo bag, and we'll call it even.
—BELA TALBOT, "FRESH BLOOD" (3-7)

Mojo bags are a pretty common element in faith magic practices, especially those of voodoo and hoodoo. Voodoo is a faith magic practice of the Caribbean Islands; hoodoo is a nearly identical practice from the southern United States.

Faith magic is a practice that manipulates and capitalizes on sacred objects, religious beliefs, and common superstitions in order to use the faith of others as a tool for healing . . . or to use against them. Like many magic practices, these can be used for either beneficial or destructive purposes. In addition to voodoo and hoodoo, also included among faith magic practices are the traditions of Santería and Espiritismo, among others.

In *Supernatural*, mojo bags are primarily used to ward off evil spirits and demons. However, their uses in faith magic are nearly limitless. There are mojo bags available for just about anything and everything—love, good luck, health, and protection against curses, just for starters. There are even mojo bags for gambling.

Getting one of these bags isn't all that hard, either. These days, you can find mojo bag vendors all over the Internet. That's right! For the incredibly low, low price of just $5.95, you, too, can be the proud owner of your very own honest to goodness mojo bag! Of course, considering the way Bela's eyes lit up when she saw Gordon's mojo bag in "Fresh Blood" (3-7), it is doubtful that these

Internet mojo bags are going to pack the same amount of super-natural punch.

DEVIL'S SHOESTRING

Y'see, I noticed something in your hotel room. Something tucked above the door—an herb. Devil's Shoestring. Well there's only one use for that . . . holding hellhounds at bay.

—DEAN WINCHESTER, "TIME IS ON MY SIDE" (3-15)

In "Time Is on My Side" (3-15), Dean spies an herb hanging over the hotel room door of *Supernatural* con artist Bela Talbot. She hangs this "herb," which is actually a plant (or the root of a plant) called Devil's Shoestring, over her door because it is commonly used in a number of spiritual and magical practices as a charm to ward off evil spirits and demons. So one might say it is not 100 percent accurate, according to available lore, when Dean Winchester claims that "there's only one use for that."

There are many spells and rituals that incorporate the Devil's Shoestring root, which serve a variety of purposes, far too many to cover them all here. However, below is a summary of at least one common version of a pseudo-Judeo-Christian ritual that involves the use of this root and is said to ward off demons and malevolent spirits. Various similar rituals can be found in Wicca and certain forms of faith magic.

1. Immerse the Devil's Shoestring root completely in holy water for roughly twelve to twenty-four hours.

2. Remove it from the water and allow it to dry.

3. Recite the short version of the prayer to Saint Michael the Archangel (see chapter 4) and tie the root into the shape of a cross (commonly by using a red string).

4. Once the prayer is completed and the cross shape has been securely tied into place, you then hang the Devil's Shoestring cross over the main entryway of the house, room, or domicile.

There is a more generic use of Devil's Shoestring in folklore, which claims that shoving it into the ground in front of the threshold of a door will "trip up the devil." This "tripping" of the devil is where the root gets its name, in that it trips up the devil in the same way that humans are sometimes tripped up by their own shoelaces.

Of course, the effectiveness of weapons is limited when it comes to dealing with beings that come from "across the veil." Many of the tools that are used by hunters in *Supernatural* deal with manipulating paranormal forces. From summoning to prophecy, let us look at the various *Supernatural* elements that serve to pierce the veil between this world and the next.

≡ 2 ≡

SIGNS, VISIONS, SEALS, AND SIGILS

I n this chapter we are going to take a look at some of the various elements, items, and characters from the *Supernatural* mythos that involve communicating with and/or manipulating spiritual and supernatural forces. From prophets and seers to sigils and seals, these are the ways in which the Winchesters "pierce the veil" between this world and the next.

PROPHETS

Since ancient, possibly even prehistoric, times there have been special human beings who have what some refer to as a "second sight." They are able to see beyond the veil that separates this world from the next. Seers, soothsayers, and prophets have played a long and significant part in human history. While there are many different types of special individuals who are in one way or another able to foresee events to come, they usually fall into three primary categories:

1. **Prophet Scribes:** These are prophets who transcribe their revelations in written form (such as Enoch . . . and Chuck).

2. **Seers:** These individuals experience visions, often not by any conscious control, of events to come.

3. **Divine "Receivers":** These sorts of prophets receive direct divine instructions and revelations from either God or an agent of God (most commonly an angel).

CHUCK AND THE PROPHET SCRIBE ENOCH

I am the prophet . . . Chuck!
—CHUCK SHURLEY, "THE MONSTER AT
THE END OF THIS BOOK" (4-18)

The *Supernatural* character Chuck Shurley would certainly fall into the category of a prophet scribe since he writes everything he foresees into his books (well, he writes down almost everything . . . he left out some stuff, like when Sam was drinking demon blood). To be honest, Chuck has a lot in common with one of the oldest prophet scribes in religious mythology, Enoch, author of the book of Enoch. While this text is considered apocryphal (or "unauthorized") by most Judeo-Christian traditions, it is obvious that much of its writings influenced later works of Judaic lore.

Aside from offering a very thorough account of the cosmological order, the book of Enoch (believed to have been written sometime around 300 BCE, but likely originated from a much older myth that may have been passed along via a verbal tradition long before it was permanently written down) also offers the most complete chronological account of the war in Heaven and the fall of the rebel angels. On the whole, this text claims to be a written account of the divine visions and experiences of the prophet scribe Enoch, father of the Jewish leader Methuselah. Enoch was also an ancestor of Noah, who preserved life and Judaic civilization with his ark during the Great Deluge of the Old Testament.

In the book of Enoch, a group of angels take Enoch to the heavens and reveal to him the truth behind the great mysteries of existence. Enoch learns of the "Oneness" of God, an idea very similar to the monotheism of Judaism. He also learns of the arrangements of the hierarchy of Heaven and Earth. He even witnesses the exile of the rebel angels. In fact, when these angels are judged it is Enoch who is sent to inform them of God's coming wrath. Interestingly, these angels even beg Enoch to make an appeal to God on their behalf. But it is futile, as God's judgment is final and absolute.

Like Enoch, Chuck Shurley also deals with angels on a regular and very personal basis. And like Enoch, Chuck writes all that he foresees in the form of stories. Lastly, Chuck is rarely able to do anything to stop that which he has foreseen, just as Enoch was unable to stay God's wrath against the rebel angels.

TIRESIAS: THE BLIND SEER

The second category of prophet is best exemplified by a character from Greek mythology, the blind seer Tiresias. Despite being blind, Tiresias always saw the truth of matters (even when he wished he did not). Many heroes of Greek mythology would seek out and consult with Tiresias in moments of crisis. Unfortunately, his news was rarely if ever good. So, you might say Tiresias was a lot like the blind psychic Pamela Barnes of *Supernatural*, who had her eyes burned out when she looked upon the true visage of Castiel in "Lazarus Rising" (4-1).

Probably one of the best-known tales from Greek mythology involving Tiresias comes from Homer's *Odyssey*. Oddly enough, Tiresias is already dead at this point. However, in order to find his way back home, the wayward hero Odysseus must travel into the underworld to consult with the soul of the dead prophet. Odysseus and his crew make the harrowing journey, and he uses a blood offering ritual (taught to him by the sea witch Circe, after a bit of aggressive encouragement) to draw out Tiresias's spirit. However, little of what he learns of the true state of his home is good news: his wife is being pursued by indulgent and dishonorable suitors, who believe he is dead; his son is unable to protect the home in Odysseus's absence; and his father is dead. The good news? He learns how to get home, just in time for a little payback—so there's a silver lining, after all. Unfortunately for Pamela, her silver lining came only in the afterlife, which, luckily for her, was a lot better than the dark realm of Hades in which Tiresias ended up.

MOSES OF THE ISRAELITES

I think we can rule Moses out as a suspect.

—CASTIEL, "THE THIRD MAN" (6-3)

Moses is perhaps the single most important figure in the history of Judaism and is a great example of a divine "receiver" type of prophet. Born in a time when the Israelites were supposedly in captivity to the Egyptians, Moses was actually raised among the Egyptians. Fearing for her newborn son's life, his Hebrew birth mother set him adrift on the Nile, and he was found and adopted by the wife of the pharaoh. Later, Moses learns of his true Hebrew lineage and grows enraged when he sees how his people are treated. In a fit of rage at seeing a Hebrew being beaten by an Egyptian, Moses kills the Egyptian and has to flee Egypt. However, as Judaic mythology tells us, he would one day return to Egypt to set the wrong things right.

Eventually, Moses receives divine instructions in the form of a burning bush that is not consumed by the surrounding flames. He is tasked with the mission of leading the Hebrews out of Egypt. With a staff that he can transform at will into a serpent, Moses goes before the pharaoh and demands that the Hebrews be released. The pharaoh, of course, refuses, and God unleashes a series of terrible plagues upon Egypt until the pharaoh complies. Moses eventually leads the Hebrews out of Egypt to the holy land (Israel), a place that, sadly enough, he does not live to see with his own eyes. One day, Moses ascends to the mountaintop and never comes back down. According to Judaic lore, Moses would die before seeing God's promised land because of an impulsive act of frustration in which he struck a rock with his staff.

Speaking of Moses's staff, it's a good thing Sam and Dean were able to get that thing back before the rest of the Plagues of Egypt were unleashed once more.

SIGILS AND SEALS

Religious magic and Judeo-Christian mysticism both play large parts in the mythos of *Supernatural*, and the series is saturated with the use of sigils, symbols, and materials that are related to these ancient practices. In fact, nearly every spell, conjuration, sigil, and symbol that is used on the show can be traced back to a number of very real origins.

A sigil is broadly defined as a sign, symbol, or image that is meant to possess magical powers or supernatural properties. By this definition, the term *sigil* can be broadly applied to just about any magical symbol. However, when these sigils are used for confining or blocking certain powers or entities, they would be more accurately referred to as *seals*. A large number of sigils and seals appear on *Supernatural*, so many that to fully explain them all would take a hundred pages at best. However, here is a brief list summarizing some of the most significant sigils and seals that have appeared on the show:

- **Sigil of Satan/"Pitchfork" Seal:** Lucifer traces this pitchfork or trident shaped symbol on an icy window in the season 5 finale. It was also carved into the flesh of a possessed man by Crowley in "Born under a Bad Sign" (2-14), creating a binding seal to prevent the demon from vacating the body. In Christianity, some view this sigil's three-pronged fork as a symbol of the demonic forces of Lucifer, which oppose the Christian Trinity.

SUPERNATURAL FACTS

The identity of the yellow-eyed demon who killed Mary Winchester (thus setting her husband and young sons on their paranormal paths to destiny) wasn't revealed until "In My Time of Dying" (2-1). Even in this episode, however, his name was not spoken. Instead, John Winchester used a summoning ritual to force the yellow-eyed demon to appear so he could strike a deal to save Dean's life. As a part of this ritual John chalked a symbol on the floor. Intuitive fans who saw this then researched the sign, which turned out to be the Seal of Saturn, also known as the Sigil of Azazel. So it would seem that the fans figured out Azazel's name several episodes before it was actually spoken. Needless to say, the fandom of *Supernatural* is nothing if not inquisitive.

- **Tibetan Tulpa Sigil:** This sigil, shown in the episode "Hell House" (1-17), is from the written language Sanskrit, adapted into Tibetan script, and is a combination of three phonetic symbols—*tsa*, *la*, and *pa*—to create the word *tulpa*. The sigil alone, as portrayed on *Supernatural*, is not actually complete. It is just part of the wording and chants used to create a *tulpa*, or "thought-form." Separate groups of monks chant while collectively concentrating on three different forms of energy—*dang* (combined inner and outer energy), *rolpa* (visual energy), and *tsal* (physical/real energy)—and focus this energy upon an idea or object until they all combine to create a physical object. Usually, these objects are small, such as a cup or piece of fruit. Rarely would Tibetan monks attempt to create a living animal or person, and being pacifists, they would most definitely not manifest a homicidal, hatchet-wielding spirit.

- **Angel-banishing Sigil:** While this sigil is mainly just a fabrication of the *Supernatural* mythos, it does incorporate symbols from the Enochian alphabet (more on this later in this chapter). The combination of a triangle atop a circle is correctly symbolic of the sigil's purpose, however. An upturned triangle commonly symbolizes Heaven or the divine realm, whereas the circle stands for the Earth and/or its elements. So it would stand to reason that these shapes would be combined in a sigil meant to temporarily banish angels back to Heaven.

- **Sigil of Baphomet:** In the episode "Malleus Maleficarum" (3-9), the "book club" coven of dark witches use an altar to summon demonic powers. The black altar cloth they use bears a symbol of an inverted pentagram containing the head of a goat. This symbol has long been a part of dark magic and demonic worship, representing Baphomet. The irony is that the demon Baphomet was invented by the Christian church around the sixteenth century, during its campaigns against European pre-Christian pagan (a word that actually means "country people") religions.

THE *KEY OF SOLOMON*

SAM: Bobby . . . this book . . . I've never seen anything like it.
BOBBY: The *Key of Solomon*? It's the real deal, all right.
—SAM WINCHESTER AND BOBBY SINGER, "DEVIL'S TRAP" (1-22)

In the Judeo-Christian tradition, King Solomon was the oldest son of the legendary King David (yes, as in the guy from the David and Goliath story). The story goes that God offered Solomon a choice between one of two gifts—wisdom or unlimited riches. He, of course, chose wisdom and because of this was both wise and extremely wealthy.

Solomon's father, King David, had received a prophecy from God that he would die on a Sabbath day. A Sabbath was considered an unfortunate day to die, because it was an ordered day of rest according to the law. This meant that anyone who died on a Sabbath would not receive burial rites until the day was over. David spent sunrise to sunset of every Sabbath studying God's law in order to avoid this fate, knowing that the angel of death, Azrael, would not take the soul of a man at such a sacred time. Azrael, however, caused David to hear sounds of commotion in the nearby palace garden. David went to investigate. As he descended the garden stairs, Azrael caused them to collapse and David fell to his death. King David's corpse had also fallen in a place that left it exposed to the heat of the midday sun. Solomon, who had received the gift of all knowledge and wisdom from God, used his mystical arts to summon a large number of giant eagles. The eagles flew above the corpse, offering shade and fanning the corpse so that it would not prematurely rot before it could be properly and respectfully interred in a manner befitting a king such as David.

Of course, Solomon could do a lot more with his divine gift than summon a bunch of big eagles. Among Solomon's abilities was the knowledge of summoning and controlling spirits, both angels and demons alike. By standing inside magical symbols and circles of protection, the most well-known among these being the Seal of Solomon, he was able to summon powerful demons and spirits while being protected from them. If Solomon was given all knowledge and wisdom, then it would stand to reason that he could read and write. This leads one to assume that he would have written down what he knew. The text in which Solomon supposedly wrote down the symbols he used for conjurations and protection is referred to as the *Key of Solomon*.

Over the years, a number of people have stepped forward claiming to have been told the secrets of the original *Key of Solomon* text. However, it is important to note that no such ancient text has ever been discovered or verified. The first of these *Key of Solomon* manuscripts began to appear around the fifteenth century, and continued well into the twentieth century. One of the last persons to come forward with what he claimed to be the true *Magical Treatise of Solomon* was Armand Delatte, who published his version of the manuscript in 1927. To this day, Delatte's text is widely considered no more than a fabrication.

Between the sixteenth and eighteenth centuries, a number of new individuals came forward claiming to have viewed and/or copied all or part of the *Key of Solomon*. While many of these texts have similar magical symbols in them, and cover many of the same topics, none of them are 100 percent the same. Most of these manuscripts were likely just imitations of mystical texts kept by Jewish adherents of Kabala or similar Arabic mystics, who were popularly hired as healers and advisers by many medieval nobles of the period.

SUPERNATURAL FACTS

The seal used to trap the demon Meg in Bobby Singer's house in the *Supernatural* episode "Devil's Trap" (1-22) is actually a combination of two symbols taken from existing versions of the *Key of Solomon*. The symbol's outer section uses parts from the Seal of Solomon, and the interior is filled by a scorpion, or "the Fifth Pentacle of Mars," in the same text. This may have been done in order to show that Bobby Singer's *Key of Solomon* was the genuine article, since these symbols are not combined in any of the other known manuscripts of that text (as already stated, none of the known texts of the *Key of Solomon* are considered authentic).

The questionable nature of the various *Key of Solomon* texts explains why, in *Supernatural*, Bobby says, "It's the real deal, all right." Sam and Dean, considering their upbringing, would likely have been familiar with the controversy surrounding this book, but they would have also known that most if not all of the texts were frauds or, at best, incomplete imitations of an original text. So Bobby would need to confirm that the book Sam was reading was the *actual Key of Solomon*.

ENOCHIAN WARDING MAGIC

I followed him. It's not far, but . . . it's layered in Enochian warding magic. I can't get in.
—CASTIEL, "ABANDON ALL HOPE" (5-10)

The word *Enochian* is used a lot on *Supernatural*, and yet not much detail is provided as to what this word means or where it comes from. While the written language of Enochian is not something that the writers of *Supernatural* just made up, neither is it exactly what one could classify as a "real" magical or divine language.

The alphabet was first introduced back in the sixteenth century by a pair of gentlemen named John Dee and Sir Edward Kelley. Dee was what you might call a supernatural jack-of-all-trades—astrologer, mystic, magician, and occultist—he had his hand in just about everything. Apparently, Dee's lifelong search for power and occult wisdom left him wanting. Eventually, he hooked up with a shady fellow named Sir Edward Kelley. Many scholars view Kelley, whose real last name was actually Talbot, as little more than a con man who used illusion and tricks to swindle money and gifts out of the far wealthier John Dee.

Dee and Kelley began using trance states in order to invoke a type of "voluntary possession" that would allow them to communicate with divine or spiritual beings. Since he claimed to have the most experience between the two of them, Kelley acted as the spirit medium during these sessions. Eventually, something supposedly came calling and took possession of Kelley, though most believe that he just started "performing" for Dee so as not to lose his wealthy benefactor's favor, enthusiasm, or, perhaps most importantly, his money.

SUPERNATURAL FACTS

Does the name Talbot sound familiar to you? It should. *Supernatural*'s most notorious paranormal con artist is a crafty young lady named Bela Talbot. Bela's last name was likely chosen because of the fact that many of today's occultists and paranormal researchers view Edward Talbot (aka Sir Edward Kelley) as a con man who used tricks and theatrics to swindle money out of the rich and naïve.

John Dee began to write down the information dictated to him by Kelley, who had successfully convinced Dee that angels were speaking through him. One of the first things that these "angels" told to Dee (through Kelley, of course) was an alphabet, which they called Enochian. According to Dee's later writings, this alphabet was used for communication between angels and certain humans. This would explain why they called it Enochian—the ancient scribe Enoch, author of a pre-Judaic text commonly known as the book of Enoch, is written of as having communicated directly with the angels of the "Lord of Spirits," likely an ancient title for God. It is definitely not outside the realm of plausibility that Edward Kelley was familiar with the existence of the book of Enoch.

Kelley sometimes wrote the symbols out for Dee, first claiming that he heard a series of taps that caused him to see in his mind's eye both the symbols as well as the sounds they represented. Interestingly enough, these symbols had dual meanings. Each symbol was attached to both a word as well as one or more phonetic sounds. One point of controversy, which many people see as evidence that Kelley made up the whole Enochian alphabet, is that these symbols conveniently represent all of the letters in the English alphabet. This allowed the angels to convey messages to Dee and Kelley through the English language.

SUPERNATURAL FACTS

In "My Bloody Valentine" (5-14) the hearts of two lovers who die in a suicide pact are marked with an Enochian symbol that resembles a heart. In the Enochian alphabet, this is the symbol for *Nach/h*. In fact, Castiel speaks Enochian to force out Cupid, the cherub angel who made these marks, and can be heard saying "Nach" near the end of this incantation.

Eventually, Kelley claimed that he was able to visually communicate with the angels through the use of a crystal. This cut down on the time needed to complete their sessions, since up to this point Dee and Kelley had no choice but to decipher the letters by listening to series of taps. Kelley claimed that by looking into the crystal he could see the angels, who would open their mouths and remove small slips of paper. Upon these were written messages, pieces of "secret" information. Oddly enough, these messages were not in Enochian but instead written in English, adding yet another suspicious inconsistency.

The Enochian alphabet, as written down by Dee and Kelley, contains twenty-two symbols/letters (for more on the significance of the number 22, see chapter 3), which are listed below with both their letter name and English equivalent:

1. Ceph/z
2. Don/r
3. Drux/n
4. Fam/s
5. Gal/d
6. Ged/g and j
7. Ger/q
8. Gisg/t
9. Gon/i
10. Gon (with point)/ w and y
11. Graph/e
12. Mals/p
13. Med/o
14. Nach/h
15. Or/f
16. Pal/x
17. Pa/b
18. Tal/m
19. Un/a
20. Ur/l
21. Van/u and v
22. Veh/c and k

⇛ 3 ⇚

A CRASH COURSE IN DEMONOLOGY

O n the night of November 2, 1983, the yellow-eyed demon Azazel took the life of a young mother named Mary Winchester. Her husband, John, would spend the rest of his life hunting down that demon, all the while raising their young sons to be skilled supernatural hunters who could continue his mission should he fail. Years later, when a soul contract between a crossroads demon and one of those sons, Dean Winchester, expires, Dean's body is torn to shreds and his soul is dragged off to Hell by Lilith's demonic hellhounds. Needless to say, demons play a key role in the mythology of the *Supernatural* universe, but where did the dark spirits we call demons come from and, perhaps more importantly, what are they?

DEMONS OF OLD

The concept of demons is not as old as one might think. In actuality, most ancient civilizations did not even have a word for demon. There were certainly spirits and gods that represented negative or destructive forces, but these forces were commonly considered a necessary part of the balance of the cosmic order. There are people who hold the mistaken belief that the notion of demons originated with the Judeo-Christian ideas regarding Lucifer or "fallen angels." This is not entirely correct, either. The demonology of Judaism has a number of malevolent entities that predate Lucifer's fall in the mythical chronology. Lucifer aside, many of the figures now referred to as demons have their origins in preexisting, sometimes even prehistoric, religious traditions.

ZOROASTER'S DEMONS: DAEVAS

DEAN: What's a daeva?

SAM: It translates to "demon of darkness." Zoroastrian demons, and they're savage, animalistic. You know, nasty attitudes—kind of like demonic pit bulls.

—SAM AND DEAN WINCHESTER, "SHADOW" (1-16)

Daevas first came onto the scene in *Supernatural* in "Shadow" (1-16), when the troublesome demon Meg summons them to kill the Winchester brothers and draw out their father, John. The "daeva sigil" used on the show is definitely a fabrication, but it is interesting to note that it resembles a Z, likely in reference to the prophet Zoroaster, the founder of the Zoroastrianism tradition and from whom the religion gets its name (for more, see chapter 9).

Zoroaster revealed to his followers that a race of evil spirits roamed the Earth seeking the ruination of humans, often fooling the unsuspecting into worshipping them as gods. Zoroaster called these evil spirits daevas, a word he likely borrowed from the Hindu people in nearby India. According to the Hindu faith, devas are a form of benevolent intelligence, spirit, or deity. By naming his evil spirits daevas, Zoroaster was claiming that the deities of the Hindu Dharma tradition were actually evil spirits in disguise. Additionally, Zoroaster became the first to put a word to the demon concept. And this word remains in our vocabulary to this day. In fact, the modern word *devil* has its roots in the Zoroastrian word *daeva*.

According to the cosmology of Zoroastrianism, the daevas served an evil god named Angra Mainyu (or Ahriman), who opposed a benevolent god named Ahura Mazda (or Ohrmazd). For the darkness there must also be light, however. Zoroaster also explained that a race of benevolent beings, called *ahuras,* served the loving god of light Ahura Mazda (for more on this, see chapter 9). This idea likely influenced later Judaic concepts regarding angels and demons. Interestingly enough, however, it would seem that the Hindu Dharma religion did some word borrowing of its own. The word for demonic spirits in Hindu Dharma is *asura*, and it is generally believed that this word was taken from the Zoroastrian word *ahura*.

RAKSHASAS

While we're on the subject of Vedic mythology, Sam and Dean first tangled with a rakshasa disguised as a clown in "Everybody Loves a Clown" (2-2). The rakshasas were demonic beings from the Hindu Dharma mythical tradition. However, they were more like monsters than demons in that they existed in physical forms. They could change their shapes but were not said to take possession of human bodies like demons or spirits might. Their favorite food was human flesh, and male rakshasas took great enjoyment in raping both betrothed virgins and married women. The rakshasas, according to the lore, have been extinct ever since they were wiped from the face of the planet in a battle with the prince Rama, the seventh avatar of Vishnu.

The most popular tale regarding the rakshasas may be found in the Hindu epic *Ramayana* (The Power of Rama). The king rakshasa was a particularly nasty fellow named Ravana. Aside from being cruel, Ravana was also pretty crafty and cunning. Taking advantage of a boon offered by the god Shiva, Ravana asked that he and the other rakshasas be protected from being harmed by the gods and any other spiritual beings. As a result, no god or spirit, the only beings strong enough to destroy the rakshasas, could raise a hand against them (when a god makes a promise, after all, it must remain absolute). However, Ravana did not view humans as a threat and so did not include them in his deal with Shiva. This meant that a human with godlike powers would be able to destroy Ravana and his flesh-eating rakshasas without breaking Shiva's vow of divine protection.

According to the Hindu Dharma mythical tradition, the god Vishnu can come in and out of our world when he wishes, commonly by taking the form of an avatar. One such avatar was the Vedic hero Rama. Prince Rama was born to a human king who prayed to the gods for a son but was in fact an incarnation of the god Vishnu. As his Rama avatar (Vishnu has come to Earth many times as avatars; Rama being the seventh), Vishnu came to Earth in order to save humankind from the terrible reign of the rakshasas.

Rama does not attack the rakshasas unprovoked, of course, as this would be unethical of a god (even an avatar). In fact, he has to be exiled to the wild by his manipulative stepmother before he even encounters these demons. There he cuts the nose from a female rakshasa after she attacks him for refusing to give up his wife and marry the female demon. This female rakshasa just so happens to be Ravana's sister. In a fit of revenge, Ravana disguises himself as an elderly woman and tricks Rama's wife, Sita, into leaving the protection of a magic circle while her husband is away hunting. Ravana then kidnaps Sita. To rescue his wife, Rama enlists the aid of the leader of the monkeys, Hanuman, who is himself an avatar of Shiva who has also come to Earth as an avatar in order to aid Rama in destroying the rakshasas.

With Hanuman and the monkey army at his side, Rama leads an attack against Ravana's palace in order to rescue his beloved Sita and end the rakshasas' reign of terror once and for all. He slays the rakshasa king, wipes out all of the rakshasas, and rescues Sita. Then, in a less heroic manner, he nearly burns his rescued wife alive because he believes that she has been defiled by rape. Luckily, the supreme god Brahma intervenes and scolds Rama for not following his dharma (fate/role/duty) and for not trusting in his wife as she has always trusted in him. It looks like even divine avatars can make mistakes when they are restricted to a human form.

DREAMS AND NIGHTMARES: DJINN

Dean Winchester spends an entire episode under the spell of a djinni, who traps him in a dream world in which his mother is still alive ("What Is and What Should Never Be," [2-20]). While this depiction of djinn is in keeping with the Western understandings about them, their mythical portrayals are usually far more frightening.

The word *djinn* (alternatively spelled *jinn*) has actually long been used to refer to demonic spirits in the Arab world. *Djinn* is the plural form of the word, with *djinniyah* being the feminine singular and *djinni* the masculine singular form. The word *djinni* is where Westerners got the word *genie* (as in "I Dream of Jeannie"). According to the Arab mythical tradition, there are commonly five different classes of djinn, separated by how troublesome or powerful they are:

1. **Shaitan:** Referring to fallen angels, this is a transliteration of the word *Satan* (meaning "adversary").

2. **Ifrit:** Almost akin to fallen angels (in the Muslim tradition, this word actually refers to some fallen angels), this is the most troublesome type of djinn.

3. **Djinn:** While most powerful in terms of brute force, they are not quite on par with fallen angels when it comes to the scope of their powers and abilities. Apparently, there are some things that a shaitan can do that a regular djinn can't.

4. **Marid:** They aren't the most powerful, but they are the most evil and cruel type of djinn. This class revels in causing misery and ruin among humans.

5. **Jann:** The least powerful type, the jann are usually more playful in nature and are similar to tricksters. Think Aladdin, the story from *1001 Arabian Nights*. (You did *not* just think about the Disney movie!)

While the above are the accepted classes of djinn, very few myths about these desert spirits actually acknowledge to which class a djinni in a story belongs.

More than likely, the djinn carried over into the Muslim tradition from the pre-Islamic, nature-centered religious traditions of the nomadic warrior tribes of the desert known as the Bedouin. Most of the available early lore supports the idea that the djinn were originally malevolent spirits believed by the Bedouin tribes to inhabit those places considered dark, secluded, and/or accursed in the Arab world. In their earliest depictions, djinn often assumed the shapes of animals. Lore also claims that djinn could render their forms invisible, or appear and move as clouds of mist.

When the Islamic religion came to dominate the Middle East, the djinn were integrated into the new religious mythology. This did, however, cause the lore to undergo some changes. Djinn were no longer portrayed as purely malevolent. In fact, post-Islamic djinn were sometimes depicted as having capacities for both good and evil. Their likenesses also lost many of the animal traits, often becoming more humanlike in appearance. But the animal traits did not disappear entirely. For example, the female djinniyah might be described as having the face and body of a human woman. Their hands or feet, however, would be replaced with cloven goat hooves or panther paws that revealed their true natures. Often, djinn would also sport serpentlike tails. According to post-Islamic lore, the king of the djinn is called Iblis, the Prince of Evil. Iblis is generally considered the Muslim equivalent of the Judeo-Christian figure Lucifer.

Most Westerners are familiar with djinn owing to the Aladdin story in *1001 Arabian Nights*. However, few are aware that djinn appeared to the Judeo-Christian king Solomon (a character also included in Islamic lore), who was at first filled with terror by their terrifying countenances. Because of his God-given wisdom, however, Solomon was able to overcome his fear, and eventually he became a master over the djinn and was able to capitalize on the abilities of these powerful spirits and use them to his benefit.

THE TRUTH ABOUT SAMHAIN

Among the pre-Christian demons encountered by the Winchester boys, there was a mean little number by the name of Samhain who was summoned by a warlock wearing a high school art teacher as a meat suit and his homicidal witch of a sister, who was wearing a cheerleader—very fashionable ("It's the Great Pumpkin, Sam

Winchester," [4-7]). Unlike the daevas and djinn, which have Middle Eastern origins, the concept of Samhain comes to us from Europe. While the Samhain portrayed in *Supernatural* is a demonic entity, Samhain's nature isn't quite that simple to explain.

Many believe that Samhain is the name of a pre-Christian Celtic death god. Technically speaking, however, Samhain isn't the name of any supernatural entity; it is neither a god nor a demon. Instead, Samhain refers to a specific time of year. The word actually means "the End of Summer."

The misinterpretation about Samhain is thought to have occurred sometime during the eighteenth century and was likely caused by the fact that Celts celebrated a feast of Samhain. Among other rites and prayers, the festival involved a ritual in which a corncob doll was ceremonially thrown into a fire by a rider on horseback being chased by two other riders who pretended to be trying to stop him or her. The burning of the corncob doll was a symbol of the seasonal death of the fertility god, who would be resurrected once more at the arrival of spring. As often happens in mythological studies, an early academic text misinterpreted a single piece of information, claiming that Samhain was a Celtic god of death, and then later texts cited this initial piece of misinformation as a source. This trend continued until the initial misinformation became widely accepted as a valid fact.

LUCIFER

Luci! I'm hoooooooooome!

—GABRIEL, "HAMMER OF THE GODS" (5-19)

Whether you're talking about demons or fallen angels, Lucifer is the undisputed alpha dog in the room. The name Lucifer actually means "light bringer," but the name has also been commonly translated as "morning star" or "morning light." In ancient Judaism, spiritual beings such as angels were often associated with celestial bodies. It is generally thought that Lucifer was at one point associated with the planet Venus. Some others even claim that he may have been a preexisting solar deity, but there is little concrete evidence to support this theory. Lucifer's name later came to be interpreted as a reference to his fall from Heaven. The former angel's fall from grace is commonly said to have resembled a fiery star falling from the sky.

One of the biggest misconceptions about Lucifer is that his name is literally Satan. The word *Satan* is actually more of a title than a name and translates as something like "adversary" or "enemy"; this term is in no way exclusive to the fallen angel Lucifer. A number of demonic entities (and even certain "accusing angels" of the early Judaic tradition, before they added demons to their mythical tradition) are also referred to as Satan. Basically, the word is used to refer to demons as enemies or adversaries of God and humankind. Satan can also have a more figurative meaning, used in reference to the internal conflict of good versus evil that occurs within the human soul. Mistranslations of the word *Satan* have led to a number of mistaken conclusions regarding certain verses in Judeo-Christian texts.

There are a number of differing versions regarding the "what" and "why" of how Lucifer got his icy butt booted out of Heaven, especially when it comes to the nature of his rebellion—namely, why he rebelled. The one common element that remains the same across nearly the entire board is the fact that Lucifer began his existence as the single most beautiful, powerful, and beloved of all God's angels. His domain was the entire night sky, from dusk to dawn, and his abilities far exceeded those of his angelic brothers (considering that night is seen as contrary to the warmth of day, this may explain why certain parts of lore claim that Lucifer is "icy" by nature).

At some point, however, Lucifer was no longer content with the many gifts he'd been given. This is where the various stories about him start to differ. Some myths claim that the war began when Lucifer refused to bow to God's new creation, humans, after being commanded to do so (as you'll see in chapter 8 on Lilith, the Old Testament God could get pretty creative with the whole "wrath thing" when he was disobeyed). Others claim that Lucifer's anger stemmed from the fact that God gave humans souls and free will, both of which had been denied to angels. Most Christians will tell you that Lucifer believed he was more powerful than God, though you'll have a hard time finding that directly explained in the Christian Bible. For the most part, the Christian lore (in the canonical texts, anyway) basically says that Lucifer rebelled owing to his pride. However, if Lucifer's indignant feelings were due to humans being given free will, something he'd been denied, then this poses an interesting question—how does an angel rebel against God if he/it does not have free will?

Using his beauty and radiance, and offering them promises of power and glory, Lucifer was able to convince a third of Heaven's angels (though not all versions of the myth support this estimate) to join him in rebellion against their father and creator, God. The rebellious angels, according to the story in the book of Enoch, numbered two hundred. As everyone knows, the battle did not end well for Lucifer or his angel coconspirators. When the war in Heaven neared its end, Judeo-Christian lore claims that God himself had to intervene. Michael was given the same powers as Lucifer and, with God's favor, was able to defeat and subdue his rebellious brother. Lucifer was shown no mercy as he was judged for his blasphemous betrayal. The once highest of all angels was then stripped of all angelic titles, which were replaced with the shameful title of Satan, and the former angel of light was cast into the realm of suffering known as *Sheol*.

Sheol refers to a pit or an abyss of death and suffering. When the Christian Bible was first translated into Greek, the word *Sheol* was mistranslated to words such as *Hades* (Lord of the Underworld) or *Necropolis* (City of the Dead). When the Bible was later translated from Greek to English, the word was translated as *Hell*, which was an alternative spelling of Hel, the name of the Saxon and Norse goddess of the underworld and death.

Oddly enough, Christians often believe that Lucifer was condemned to a horrible prison in an actual place called Hell. However, this is not exactly the Judaic tradition's view on the matter. In the Judaic interpretation (further supported by the events documented in the book of Enoch) Lucifer and his fellow rebel angels were barred from Heaven and condemned to live in the terrible world of physical reality, of "suffering." Think of it like this: when compared to the blissful paradise of Heaven in which these angels previously resided, spending the rest of existence stuck on Earth would have been a fate worse than death. Other traditions believe that the condemned angels were imprisoned within the Earth itself. This makes sense when you compare the story to its older counterparts from the book of Enoch and the Zohar, which tell of the rebel angel Azazel being imprisoned beneath the sands of a desert called Dudael for corrupting humans with indulgent knowledge and destructive technology.

DEMONS AND FALLEN ANGELS

One thing you need to know is that not all demons are former/fallen angels. As you read earlier, many are actually the demonized versions of deities from preexisting religions. Simply put: while all fallen angels are categorized as demons, not all demons are fallen angels. Interestingly enough, it would seem that the creators of *Supernatural* are aware of this. When one looks at the eye color of the different demons on *Supernatural*, it becomes clear that these colors are designations of demon types. Consider the following list:

1. **White Eyes:** Demons with white eyes are malevolent demonic figures that come from pre-Judaic or pre-Christian traditions, such as Lilith (see chapter 8), Samhain, and Alastair.

2. **Colored Eyes:** Colored eyes, excluding red, black, and white, designate fallen angels, such as the yellow-eyed Aza-

zel. As of the early episodes of season 6, Lucifer has not yet revealed any special eye color (though in some of the online *Supernatural* fan fiction, writers have speculated in their stories that Lucifer's eyes are blue or amethyst in color).

3. **Red Eyes:** This eye color appears to be exclusive to crossroads demons (more on these former colleagues of *Supernatural's* Crowley in just a moment). However, it is interesting to note that Crowley, self-proclaimed "King of the Crossroads," was never portrayed with red eyes.

4. **Black Eyes:** Black eyes denote lower-order demons, which are the corrupted souls of humans that have been transformed by the evil influences of Lucifer or from spending too long in the torments of Hell.

The most interesting addition *Supernatural* makes to preexisting demonic lore is the idea that human souls can turn into demons as a result of the corrupting influence of living in Hell. Ideas similar to this can be found in certain Eastern mythical traditions but are not commonly found in Judeo-Christian traditions. For example, in Japanese Shinto lore, a human who is murderous or takes joy in violence can transform into a demonlike creature called an *oni*. One demonic concept that has been around for thousands of years, however, is the crossroads demon.

So . . . what's your soul worth?

A FIDDLE OF GOLD
AGAINST YOUR SOUL

You know, I usually like to be warned before I'm violated by demon tongue.

—DEAN WINCHESTER, "CROSSROAD BLUES" (2-8)

Crossroads demons, or similar mythical concepts and superstitions, have been around pretty much as long as there have been roads that cross. Crossroads lore is surprisingly universal and can be found in cultures from Europe, Greece, India, ancient Mongolia, Japan, and Native America. The list of supernatural beings to be found at crossroads varies from one culture to another but includes angry spirits, witches, sprites, ancestral ghosts, fairies, and (you guessed it) demons. Some cultures used crossroads as burial spots for the undesirable dead, such as murderers, thieves, and suicides. Others reserved crossroad burials for the bodies of parricides (those who were guilty of murdering one or both of their parents). In post-Christian medieval lore crossroads were the meeting places of witches, who would use them to conduct their dark ceremonies.

In the *Supernatural* episode "Crossroad Blues," Sam and Dean make a reference to the musician Robert Johnson selling his soul to the devil in order to become the greatest blues musician in the world. Believe it or not, this story has been around for a long time. Whether true or not, during his time Robert Johnson did become the greatest blues musician in the world.

Robert Johnson was born May 8, 1911 or 1912 (new evidence

has called his birth year into question), in Hazlehurst, Mississippi. His mother, Julia Dodds, was the wife of a wealthy plantation owner named Charles Dodds. Problem was, Robert's biological father wasn't Charles, but a man named Noah Johnson. As a baby, Robert's mother was chased out of Hazlehurst by a lynch mob. Some say it was due to a quarrel her husband had with some white plantation owners. Others claim it was because her husband found out that the child wasn't his. Regardless of why she was run out of town, she took Robert with her. Two years later, she sent the boy to Memphis, Tennessee, to live with her husband who had, for some reason, changed his name to Charles Spencer. Many believe that it was in Memphis that Robert was first exposed to the blues.

In 1919, when Robert was eight (or seven) years old, his mother had remarried, this time to a *much* younger man named Dusty Willis. She sent for Robert to come live with her in Robinsonville, Mississippi. According to the stories, it was at this time that Robert also began following around a legendary blues musician named Son House, trying to learn from him. House, however, did not see any special talent in the enthusiastic young boy. Robert received a formal education during this time and lived in Robinsonville until 1929. This was also the year Robert married Virginia Travis, who died shortly after during childbirth. This is also where the story starts to get just a little weird.

After his wife's death, Robert disappeared. No one knows where he went or what transpired during his absence. Only a few months later, however, he reappeared—with an incredible new guitar technique, the likes of which had never been seen before.

No one knows where he learned it, but the story goes something like this:

When Johnson went missing, people said he found work on a Mississippi plantation, most likely the Dockery Plantation. While there, his grief over the loss of his wife led him back to his love of the blues, and he decided he would become a great blues musician. After consulting with a local hoodoo-voodoo mambo (kind of like a priestess), he was told to take his guitar to a crossroads near the plantation and start playing. Once at the crossroads, Johnson had barely struck a chord when he was met by a very large and well-dressed black man (perhaps Baron Samedi? See chapter 9). This man, whom the lore claims was the devil himself, took the guitar from Johnson, tuned it, and began to play. He then offered the guitar back to Johnson, who took it with the knowledge that this was a deal with the devil, and that the collateral was his soul. Johnson took back his guitar (sorry, no awkwardly homoerotic kiss to seal the deal in this story), and with it he gained musical ability that was far beyond that of any blues guitar player ever before. His ability would make him famous in his time as well as that of future generations who rediscovered his music in the 1960s.

Johnson even toured with the man who had once not believed he possessed the necessary talent to become a great blues man— Son House. In fact, many believe that it was Johnson and House who likely began spreading the "crossroad pact" story. House may have even believed it, some theorize, in order to explain how Johnson achieved such an extreme amount of guitar ability in what seemed like such an impossibly short amount of time. If the story is true, of course, Johnson's dream of becoming the greatest blues musician in the world also came with a very hefty price: his soul.

And the weirdness continues. Johnson died young, at the age of only twenty-seven (or twenty-six). His death also came under very odd circumstances on August 16, 1938, only nine years after his supposed crossroad pact. Of course, there is nothing in a pact that says the person giving up his body cannot die and have his soul collected sooner than the contract's expiration date. Sometimes, the devil might even find a way to help you along. And, for Robert Johnson, it would seem the devil was doing a little nudging.

A few days before his death, Johnson had been playing for a rural country dance hall in Greenwood, Mississippi. After his set was over, Johnson took a seat. The bar owner sent over an open bottle of whiskey, compliments of the house. For reasons unknown (though some say it was because Johnson was flirting with the bar owner's woman), the whiskey had been laced with strychnine, a very potent poison (and, in small doses, a hallucinogen). As he raised the bottle, fellow bluesman and close friend Sonny Boy Williamson knocked the bottle from Johnson's hand. Sonny Boy then warned Johnson that it was dangerous to drink from a bottle that he didn't open himself (after all, it could be poisoned, right?). Johnson was annoyed by this and told Sonny Boy, "Never knock a bottle out of my hand." The bar owner, being the generous fellow he was, immediately sent over yet another open bottle of whiskey, laced with an equally generous amount of strychnine.

Shortly after finishing off the entire bottle of whiskey, Johnson fell suddenly ill and had to be helped back to his room. Of course, it would be safe to say that most people would need a little help getting around after drinking a whole bottle of whiskey. Over the next few days, however, Johnson's illness only worsened. He died in agonizing pain, according to those who were present, in a fit of convulsions (which, by the way, is a standard symptom of strychnine poisoning).

There are some, of course, who claim that the accounts of Johnson's poisoning death are wrong. Rationalists, such as the toxicology experts cited in Tom Graves's book *Crossroads: The Life and Afterlife of Blues Legend Robert Johnson*, claim that a fatal dose of strychnine would kill a person in hours (not several days, as in Johnson's case). Not to mention that even whiskey would be unlikely to cover the strong taste and odor of the poison. Then there are others, of course, who would say that it was not poison that killed Robert Johnson—it was the devil come to get his due.

CROWLEY: KING OF THE CROSSROADS

Let's just say, when they get their Grammy, they shouldn't all be thanking God.

—CROWLEY, "THE DEVIL YOU KNOW" (5-20)

Long before his bones were charred and he was sent packing, the *Supernatural* character Crowley, self-proclaimed "King of the Crossroads," was one of the few demonic allies the Winchesters ever had. And after their experience in their alliance with Ruby, can you blame them? However, Crowley was at least a bit more honest about his dishonesty than Ruby. While Crowley made for an interesting character, he is problematic when it comes to finding a mythical origin for him; there is no demon named Crowley, not in any legitimate demonological tradition. Still, though there may not be a mythical origin for Crowley, there is a historical one.

> BOBBY: Why'd you take a picture?
> CROWLEY: Why'd you have to use tongue?
> —BOBBY SINGER AND CROWLEY,
> "TWO MINUTES TO MIDNIGHT" (5-21)

Crowley was likely modeled after a man named Aleister Crowley, born in 1875 as Edward Alexander Crowley. It is generally believed that Crowley changed his name in order to give himself a more effective air of mystery. He took his name from the demon name of Alastor. However, he purposely changed the spelling. Using the numerical values that are given to letters in the practice of *isopsephy*, the Greek equivalent of a similar Hebrew practice of *gematria*, Crowley altered the spelling until the sum of all the letters in his name came to a total of 666, the "number of the Beast" spoken of in the Christian Bible's Revelation. Crowley even claimed to his father that he was the Beast, basically proclaiming himself the Antichrist (for more on this, see chapter 11). Apparently, plain old Alexander didn't quite have that "I'm the Antichrist" ring to it.

Opinions on Crowley vary. Some call him a self-styled mystic. Others claim that he was just a world-class con man, like Edward Talbot, who used theatrics and superstition to relieve the rich and gullible from their money. He wrote several books on "White Magick" (which include a surprising number of ceremonies that require sexual acts). But Crowley wasn't into one kind of magic. He was into *all* kinds of magic. To be honest, most who are familiar with his work agree that if he had come across any dark forces that would give him powers, he would have taken them. Considering Crowley's background as a swindler, a mystic, and the kind of man who lusts for power, the name is certainly fitting of the *Supernatural* character.

SUPERNATURAL FACTS

Dean Winchester is a big Led Zeppelin fan. Believe it or not, guitarist Jimmy Page was obsessed with the work of Aleister Crowley. Page even purchased Crowley's former estate, the Boleskine House, which was used to film certain fantasy sequences in the band's film *The Song Remains the Same*.

For some time fans speculated that the demon Alastair, who tortured Dean Winchester in Hell, was based on Aleister Crowley. When the crossroads demon Crowley came on the scene, however, these theories were proven wrong. This may have even been the reason for naming Crowley as they did, so that fans would have to look again. The mythical origins of Alastair will be discussed later in this chapter.

AZAZEL: THE YELLOW-EYED DEMON

That was for our mom, you yellow-eyed sonuvabitch.
—DEAN WINCHESTER, "ALL HELL BREAKS LOOSE: PART 2" (2-22)

Supernatural's portrayal of Azazel, or the yellow-eyed demon as he was known for much of his time on the show, is pretty accurate when compared to the myth. However, Azazel is not exactly a demon. At least, he is not a demon like Ruby or Meg. In fact, he is a fallen angel like Lucifer. His eyes are not black, after all (or white or red, for that matter), but yellow, which fits with the idea that the fallen angels in *Supernatural* have colored eyes.

According to the ancient book of Enoch, Azazel was among those leading the charge of the rebel line when the war in Heaven broke out. Originally, he was a member of the Grigori (or Watchers) angelic order, tasked with keeping watch over humankind (as one would assume, since they are called "Watchers"). According to the text, however, Azazel wasn't content with just watching. He seems to have had a thing for messing with humans. He especially liked human women and wasn't pleased that they were supposed to be off-limits to angels (a rule that a number of other angels also seemed to have considered more of a suggestion). However, he managed to keep his extracurricular exploits on the down-low—for a little while, anyway.

After Azazel fathered children with his many human female lovers, he decided that the humans could use a little help when it came to technology, and so he taught them a vast number of new and inventive ways in which to destroy themselves. Azazel is said to have granted humans an impressive array of progressive, but ultimately self-destructive, knowledge. To human men, Azazel taught the arts of metalworking, and he showed them how to make tools to improve their quality of life and to construct weapons with which to wage war upon one another. He also wanted to make his human female lovers even more attractive (Azazel really seems to have had a thing for the ladies back in the day—a bit of a change from the nun-slaughtering maniac on *Supernatural*), so he taught women how to make and use cosmetics. At first Azazel was just banished to Earth for the trouble he caused. Unfortunately, he didn't seem to mind all that much.

His punishment was upgraded, however, when Azazel's many crimes were brought to the attention of the Lord of Light (in the book of Enoch, God is generally referred to by this name). Afraid that Azazel would only corrupt humans further, the accused Grigori was judged and punished. The archangel Raphael was given orders to confine the troublesome fallen angel in the sandy depths and bury him beneath the crushing weight of a desert called Dudael, commonly translated to mean "Despair/Isolation from God."

In "Lucifer Rising" (4-22), just before he locks them in the church and slaughters them all as sacrifices so that he can talk to the caged Lucifer, Azazel tells a roomful of nuns that he feels as if he has been, "quite literally," wandering in the "desert." More than likely, old yellow eyes is talking about his banishment to the wasteland of Dudael when he says this. The question is, of course, how did he get out? For his crimes, the book of Enoch states that Azazel will remain imprisoned beneath the sands of Dudael until the Final Judgment Day. In *Supernatural*, however, it seems that Azazel found a way to bust himself out of his cage ahead of the intended schedule.

As already explained, the Azazel of myth and demonology has a thing for messing with humans. Perhaps this is why he chose to use human children as his weapon against Heaven in *Supernatural*, using God's own creations against the angels as final weapons for Armageddon.

AZAZEL'S "SPECIAL CHILDREN"

I don't need soldiers . . . I need soldier. I just need the one.
—AZAZEL, "ALL HELL BREAKS LOOSE: PART 1" (2-21)

The powers of Azazel's "special children" vary from one individual to the next. Sam can expel demons and has psychic visions, Jake has super strength, Andy has mind control, and Ava also has visions and can control demons. Not all of their powers are so useful, however. One girl, Lily, has the unfortunate ability to kill with a touch (in fact, she tells the others that she has already accidentally killed her lesbian lover).

Regardless of what their powers are, the abilities of all of Azazel's special children manifest when they are twenty-two years of age. The number 22 has a plethora of interesting significances, any of which could be the reason the creators of *Supernatural* chose this as the age at which their powers manifest.

In the Hebraic numerological system gematria, which assigns numerical values to certain words and vice versa, the number 22 translates as *Kaph-Bet*, which (depending on how one interprets the symbols) could mean something like either "palm house" or "with the palm." The use of the number 22 in this regard may be a reference to how the most favored one of Azazel's "special children," namely Sam Winchester, sticks out his hand with his palm turned at his opponent when using his powers.

Here are some other interesting facts about the number 22 that could explain this use of the age of twenty-two for Azazel's children:

- The apocalyptic book of Revelation contains twenty-two chapters.

- In Kabala, the two Sephiroth (opposing groups of ten entities, one made up of angels and the other of demons/fallen angels) are separated by twenty-two paths.

- The Hebrew alphabet has twenty-two letters.

- All twenty-two Hebrew letters are used in Psalm 118:22: "The stone rejected by the builders has become the cornerstone."

- There are twenty-two cards in a Tarot deck.

- In numerology, where numbers have unique symbolic significances, the number 22 is the master number, called the spiritual master or master builder.

SUPERNATURAL FACTS

Azazel's "special children" were gathered in Cold Oak, South Dakota, which is, according to Sam, "the most haunted place in America." But don't plan a road trip to Cold Oak, because you won't find it: it doesn't exist.

Azazel's special children in *Supernatural* may also have origins in the book of Enoch. As already discussed, Azazel (along with a number of other angels) is said to have sired children with human women. The offspring of these unions were called Nephilim, a race of powerful and violent "giants" who wreaked havoc upon humankind. When Azazel and the other Grigori who corrupted humankind were finally punished, the Lord of Light ordered the loyal angels to wipe out the Nephilim. Since these beings had the blood of angels, perhaps some of them were able to survive this violent angelic persecution. If this was the case, then it might explain why only people of certain bloodlines are said to be able to serve as angelic vessels in *Supernatural*. The body of someone with Nephilim blood, literally making them "part angel," would likely be best suited for withstanding the immense stress of containing a powerful angel (or fallen angel, in Sam's case).

PICASSO WITH A RAZOR: ALASTAIR

The *Supernatural* character Alastair likely originated not in biblical lore, but in Greek myths. Originally, the word *alastor* was used to describe an act of justified vengeance. Eventually, however, the idea was personified and become the name of a dark and menacing figure similar to Furies (winged creatures who carried out violent justice in Greek and Roman mythology). This personification of ideas is actually not that uncommon in the realm of world mythology.

So who was Alastor? According to an 1863 demonological text by Collin de Plancy, *Dictionnaire Infernal*, Alastor is Hell's chief executioner (which makes you wonder—if people in Hell are already dead, then who is Alastor executing?). The text also says that Alastor's most dominant trait is his sadism. Torturing and killing are not just a job to Alastor. He revels in his work.

In verses 66–68 of this text, Collin de Plancy has this to say about the origins of Alastor, and his role as the "Nemesis," or an agent of justified vengeance:

> *In the infernal hierarchy, he is the Nemesis. The ancients called evil spirits "alastores." Plutarch says that Cicero hated Augustus so much that he conceived of a plan to kill himself outside Augustus' foyer, in order to become his alastor.*

The above mention of suicide is likely related to a common ancient belief that the spirits of those who commit suicide risk being transformed into demons. Another mythical element to the role of Alastair will be discussed in chapter 5.

HELLHOUNDS

I bet they could hump the crap out of your leg . . . What? They could!

—DEAN WINCHESTER, "CROSSROAD BLUES" (2-8)

First things first, hellhounds are not to be confused with the mythical concept of "black hounds." Whereas hellhounds are creatures that drag souls to the underworld (and keep them there), black hounds are death omens, primarily found in Anglo-Saxon folklore. Hellhounds are nothing new, of course. The connection between big, scary dogs and the dark horror of the underworld has been around since ancient times.

The most well-known mythical mutt to grace the gates of the underworld is the monstrous Greek creature known as Cerberus. More monster than dog, he had three heads (though some earlier texts, such as Hesiod's *Theogony*, describe Cerberus as having as many as fifty heads), a dragon's tail, and fur across his neck and upper back that was made of snakes. The creature was the off-spring of two very powerful Titans, Typhon and Echidna (in the Greek mythos, Echidna is widely considered the mother of all monsters). Considering all this, it is no wonder that the death god Hades chose to keep Cerberus as the guard dog of the underworld. Once a person had paid the underworld ferryman Charon with coins placed on the eyes of the dead for this purpose and was taken across the river Styx, however, there was still one more fee to pay.

Cerebus would tear apart any soul that attempted to pass him, whether going out or coming in. Luckily for these departed souls, Cerberus appears to have had a sweet tooth. For this reason, the dead were interred with honey-soaked cakes, or "sops," to toss to Cerberus so that he would let them pass. This led to the saying "Sop for Cerberus," whose meaning is akin to the expression "Time to pay the piper."

Eventually, the Greek hero Herakles (or Hercules) dragged Cerberus from the underworld as the last of his legendary Twelve Labors. However, Hades only allowed the hero to do so on two conditions: (1) that he used no weapons and (2) that he returned Cerberus to Hades once he'd shown the dog as proof he'd completed the task. As crazy as it sounds, Herakles accomplished the task barehanded, and even brought the monstrous mutt back once he'd plopped it at the feet of the terrified douche-of-a-king named Eurystheus as proof that he'd finished his final task. Believe it or not, Cerberus is the only monster to ever cross paths with Herakles and live to tell the tale (that is, of course, if the thing could talk . . . which would just be creepy).

Cerberus is not the only hellhound of the mythical tradition. In Egyptian myths, the death god Anubis had the black head of a dog and was aided by a monster called Ammit, which had the torso and legs of a hippopotamus and the head of a crocodile (as if normal hippos and crocs weren't bad enough, right?). In the early Vedic tradition, the death god Yama kept two dogs, Syama the Black and Sabala the Spotted, to bring and hold souls in the Purgatory-like afterlife called Naraka. Even the Norse god Odin (see chapter 9) kept a pair of wolves, Geri and Freki. During times of war, the two ravenous canines ran through the lands in order to chase down cowards, war profiteers, and dishonorable leaders, whom they quickly and violently ripped to pieces, thus giving their victims the nasty ends that were (to the Norse, at least) befitting of their actions.

CREEPY KIDS: THE ACHERI

Gimme a minute . . . I'm still working through "demons are real."

—ANDY, "ALL HELL BREAKS LOOSE: PART 1" (2-21)

An Acheri has appeared only once in *Supernatural,* during the episode "All Hell Breaks Loose: Part 1" (2-21). This is probably because the Acheri are not your typical, run-of-the-mill Judeo-Christian demons. Many early sources referred to the Acheri as being of "Indian" origin, which led newer sources to mistakenly claim that they were part of the Hindu mythical tradition, but the Acheri actually have their origins in Native American folklore. According to most of the available sources, an Acheri is an evil spirit that disguises itself as a child (almost always a young girl) and uses this ruse to infiltrate villages. Once in a village, the Acheri spreads diseases among the people.

It seems that the Acheri have a hard time maintaining their disguises in daylight, so during the day they hide, preferably near the tops of mountains. As night falls, however, they descend into nearby villages to plague mortals. More often than not, they will target the children of a village first. Whenever a child in a village fell seriously ill, it was generally blamed on an Acheri. It was said that an Acheri had "cast a shadow" upon the child. The lore also says that there is at least one way to protect oneself from the attacks of an Acheri. For some reason, an Acheri will not attack anyone who is wearing the color red anywhere on their clothing or body. This led to a practice whereby mothers began tying a red thread or scarf around the necks of their children in order to protect them from the Acheri.

As has been said, where there is darkness there must be light. And, standing in opposition to the agents of evil are the agents of good. In the Judeo-Christian traditions, these shining beacons of righteousness are commonly referred to as angels.

═ 4 ═

ANGELS . . . THEY SMITE FIRST AND ASK QUESTIONS LATER

ny fan of *Supernatural* is familiar with the angel Castiel, who gripped Dean tightly and dragged him up from the depths of Hell. Castiel is undoubtedly one of the strongest allies the Winchester brothers have. Of course, this does not mean that Sam and Dean are on 100 percent friendly terms with the other members of the angelic ranks. In fact, the angels of *Supernatural* often prove as problematic to the Winchesters as demons. As the creators of *Supernatural* have done with their portrayals of demons, they have developed a unique spin on the ancient mythos of angelology.

What are angels, exactly? Generically speaking, they could be defined as a high order of spiritual entities. No one can say for certain just how long angels have been around, but it is safe to say that they are far older than the human race. Most of the available angelic lore supports the idea that angels are a creation of God, and were brought into existence long before God created humankind. In comparison to angels, humans are often seen as being somewhat flawed.

ANGELIC ORDERS

In Judeo-Christian mythology, there exist a number of primary angelic orders. Of course, the names and numbers of these orders can differ from one tradition to the next, so this list is in no way meant to be definitive:

- **Metatron:** This is the title of a high-ranking angel who acts as the "voice of God."

- **Grigori:** These are the Watchers, many of whom the book of Enoch describes as having been cast from Heaven.

- **Archangels:** This title is held by seven of the most powerful warrior angels.

- **Seraphim:** A seraph is an angel belonging to this order, meaning "burning ones." They are commonly portrayed as having six wings and are often said to be the angelic attendants of God.

- **Cherubim:** The cherubim are led by the angel Kerubiel and are often tasked with guarding certain forbidden sites or objects, such as Eden after humanity's expulsion. Catholicism considers cherubim to be the second-highest angelic order.

CASTIEL: ANGEL OF SOLITUDE

I'm an angel of the Lord.

—CASTIEL, "LAZARUS RISING" (4-1)

The angel Castiel has been a regular figure of the *Supernatural* series ever since the concept of angels was first introduced into the mythos during the premier of season 4. Up until Castiel came on the scene, the closest the Winchester brothers had come to dealing with an angel was during season 2, episode 13, "Houses of the

SUPERNATURAL FACTS

"Houses of the Holy" is not just the title of a *Supernatural* episode. The title of this episode actually comes from a song by legendary rock band Led Zeppelin (of which Dean is undoubtedly a fan). This is not the only *Supernatural* episode to take its title from a Led Zeppelin song. The title of the episode "The Song Remains the Same" (5-13) is also the title of a Led Zeppelin song, album, and even concert film.

Holy," when they encountered the misguided rogue spirit of a dead priest who believed that he had become an avenging angel.

Having learned of humankind's darkest deeds and sinful nature while performing his confessional duties, the late priest's spirit would appear to the living and inspire them to kill a number of "evil people," all of whom were members of his own parish when he was alive. Needless to say, this priest was certainly not an angel. The case turned out to be just another angry spirit that needed "gank-ing."

This episode is also of note because we learn that at this time Dean does not believe in the existence of angels. In fact, Dean turns out to be somewhat on the fence as to whether or not he even believes there is a God. Dean tells Sam, "There's no higher power. There's no God. I mean, there's just chaos, and violence, and random unpredictable evil that comes out of nowhere and rips you to shreds." Regardless of Dean's misgivings on the existence of a divine power, after his impressive first encounter with Castiel he at least believes in angels (though he's still not exactly God's biggest fan). Of course, if an angel personally grabs you by the shoulder, forcibly drags you out of the depths of Hell, and leaves behind the very obvious mark of his palm print on your flesh, you kind of *have* to believe in angels, don't you?

Of all the angels in *Supernatural*, Castiel is undoubtedly the most popular with fans of the show. So perhaps it should not be surprising that there has been a lot of Internet chatter regarding just about everything having to do with Castiel—his name, his angelic title, you name it. Most of the Internet data available about Castiel, however, ranges from inaccurate to wrong to just plain made up.

At some point, someone somewhere posted one very misleading piece of information that claimed there was an angel Castiel in the Judaic tradition, who was an "angel of Thursday." *Supernatural* had traditionally aired on Thursdays until season 6, so fans began reposting on various fan-based websites that Castiel's name was a reference to the show's airtime. And somewhat like a *tulpa*, so many people now believe it that it's almost come to be seen as fact.

But things aren't quite that simple. Technically speaking, there is no angel named Castiel in the angelology of the Judeo-Christian tradition. More than likely, the creators of *Supernatural* altered the name of the angel Cassiel, which is the Latinized form of the Hebrew name of the angel Kafziel. Kafziel roughly translates as "God's speed" or "My speed is God."

In the traditions of both Enochian magic and Kabala mysticism, there are angels who are given specific domain over certain hours of each day of the week. If a person was looking at the angels who have domain over the hours of Thursday, Cassiel would be listed among them. But while it is true that Cassiel is one of the angels given domain over certain hours of every Thursday, he is also (depending on the time of day) technically an angel of almost every other day of the week as well.

Cassiel would seem to fit with the personality of the Castiel from *Supernatural* in that he is said to be the angel of temperance, solitude, and tears (hence Castiel's rather bland personality, by Winchester standards). When Castiel plans to trap and interrogate the archangel Raphael in the episode "Free to Be You and Me" (5-3), the mild-mannered angel reveals to Dean that he does not believe he'll survive the encounter with his former angelic comrade. When Dean asks what he plans to do with his last night on Earth, Castiel replies, "I just thought I would sit here quietly." This would certainly seem to fit the profile for an angel of temperance and solitude. Castiel is nothing if not calm, steadfast, and patient.

That is, until the most recent war in Heaven broke out after the conclusion of season 5. Lately, Castiel has been a little more stressed than is his usual.

Fans of *Supernatural* also learned in "Free to Be You and Me" that Castiel is a virgin. However, it is reasonable to assume that most, if not all, of Heaven's angels are virgins considering that, as already discussed in chapter 3, Enoch wrote that many of the fallen angels were cast down from grace because they had sex with human women.

Despite the fact that the Castiel of *Supernatural* chooses to come to Earth to intervene on Dean's behalf, this is not common of him in terms of the angel's mythological traditions. Mythologically speaking, Cassiel is unique among the angels in the sense that he rarely, if ever, intervenes in the affairs of humans (which certainly explains why Castiel is frequently portrayed on the show as being completely unfamiliar with human behavior).

In many traditions, Cassiel is said to be one of the angelic princes of the Powers. The "Powers" were the first rank of angels created by God, so you know the guy has been around for quite a while. He has dominion over the planet Saturn, and from this planet Cassiel performs his duty as a watcher or guardian angel. While certain mystical traditions have loosely associated Cassiel with the seven archangels, he is not generally considered to be among their ranks. In ancient times, he was the angel tasked with presiding over the funerary rites of kings. As far as Cassiel's angelic role is concerned, he is said to be the patron angel of tears and solitude. He comes to those who find themselves standing alone or overcome with despair, both of which certainly apply to Sam and Dean.

THE SEVEN ARCHANGELS: "HEAVEN'S BADASSES"

Different religious traditions have their own unique set of names for the seven archangels of Heaven. However, nearly all of them agree on at least four of them: Michael, Gabriel, Raphael, and Uriel. When it comes to the names of the other three archangels, things get a bit more complicated. Zachariel is also commonly listed among them (but not always). Pinning down the exact names of the final two archangels, however, is the most problematic, since they tend to change from one facet of the Judeo-Christian tradition to the next.

The book of Enoch, which would seem to be the primary text used by the creators to construct *Supernatural*'s portrayal of angels, lists the seven archangels as follows: Michael, Uriel, Gabriel, Saraqael (one of many alternative spellings of Zachariel), Raphael, Raguel, and Remiel.

Regarding the archangels, chapter 20 of the book of Enoch lists the following:

> *Uriel, one of the holy angels, who is over the world and Tartarus; Raphael, one of the holy angels, who is over the spirits of men; Raguel, one of the holy angels who takes vengeance on the world of the luminaries; Michael, one of the holy angels, to wit, he that is set over the best part of mankind and over chaos; Saraqael, one of the holy angels, who is set over the spirits, who sin in the spirit; Gabriel, one of the holy 8 angels, who is over Paradise and the serpents and the Cherubim;*

Remiel, one of the holy angels, whom God set over those who rise.

Only five potential archangels have made appearances thus far in *Supernatural*: Uriel, Michael, Zachariah/Saraqael, Raphael, and Gabriel. This is likely due to the fact that clearly identifying details regarding the remaining two can be somewhat problematic. Either way, let's take a look at the archangels of *Supernatural*.

MICHAEL: HEAVEN'S OFFICIAL "LUCIFER BUTT KICKER"

That's Michael; toughest sonuvabitch they got . . . During the last big dust up upstairs, he's the one who booted Lucifer's ass to the basement.

—BOBBY SINGER, "SYMPATHY FOR THE DEVIL" (5-1)

Fans know the archangel Michael best as an *extremely* powerful archangel, who would like nothing better than to wear Dean to the prom. When it comes to archangels, and the various religious traditions that discuss them, the opinion on Michael is pretty much the same across the board: he's the biggest, toughest angel on the block. Just about all angelic lore, regardless of the tradition or denomination that wrote it, portrays Michael as the most powerful archangel in all of creation.

There are two main ways in which the archangel Michael's name can be interpreted. The most common interpretation is "He who is as/like God (El)." In the Talmudic tradition of Judaism, his name is sometimes interpreted as the rhetorical question of "Who is as/like God (El)?"

Michael is commonly thought of as the "general" of the angels. This stems from the fact that during the war in heaven, Michael is said to have been the archangel who stepped up and led the angelic ranks into combat against the usurping angel Lucifer and his fellow rebel angels. Michael was created to lead, and his authority extends across just about every plane of existence.

As usually happens with soldiers, Michael has a lot of medals and ribbons on his chest. The archangel Michael is the chief of the Order of Virtues, as well as the Prince of the Presence (meaning God's presence). He is the patron angel of various positive attributes, such as righteousness, mercy, justice, repentance, and sanctification. On the flip side, he is also the natural enemy of evil and injustice. His most prestigious titles, however, were granted to him as a result of his loyalty and devoted service during the war in Heaven, for which God appointed Michael the angelic Prince of Israel and the holy ruler of the Fourth Level of Heaven.

Despite all these angelic titles, Michael is better known for only one: conqueror of Satan. This is because ever since the last war in Heaven, it has been Michael's angelic duty to do battle with the "great adversary" of God, namely Lucifer. In art, the archangel Michael is most commonly portrayed in this role.

For over a millennium, various artists have created visual works depicting the final moment of Michael's victory over Lucifer in battle. While these works sometimes differ in minor details, their themes are generally the same. Lucifer is usually shown on his back or stomach, and often disarmed, with his weapon lying nearby or falling out of his hand, while the archangel Michael stands over him victoriously, sometimes even pinning his rebellious brother down beneath his foot. In these depictions, Michael is often portrayed as wearing shining armor (which usually closely resembles the armor styles of the specific periods in which the works were created), pointing the tip of either a sword or spear at Lucifer's throat or chest. This scene is considered by many to be a powerful symbol of good's ultimate triumph over evil.

If ever there were a patron "angel of warriors," it would almost certainly have to be Michael. His role as an archangel has long been associated with battle, and he is almost always depicted as holding a sword or spear. While Michael is benevolent in nature, his role as a warrior often requires him to be wrathful as well. In Judaic lore, he is credited with the destruction of the ancient city of Babylon (acting under God's orders, of course).

In the book of Enoch, Michael is one of the archangels who interceded on behalf of humankind when they were suffering owing to the actions of certain rogue angels as well as their terrible human-angel offspring, the Nephilim (as discussed in chapter 3).

As is written in chapter 9 of the book of Enoch:

And then Michael, Uriel, Raphael, and Gabriel looked down from heaven and saw much blood being shed upon the earth, and all the lawlessness being wrought upon it. And they said to each other: "The earth made without inhabitant cries with a voice of crying up to the gates of heaven. And now to you, the Holy Ones of Heaven, the souls of men make appeal, saying, 'Bring our cause before the Most High.'" And they said to the Lord of Ages: 'Lord of lords, God of gods, King of kings, and Lord of Ages, the Throne of Thy glory stands unto all the generations of the ages, and Thy name holy and glorious and blessed unto all the ages! Thou who hast made all things, and hath power over all things: and all things are naked and open to Thy sight, and Thou sees all things, and nothing can hide from Thee.'

According to the Dead Sea Scrolls, which bear striking similarities to the book of Enoch, the terrible war in Heaven is referred to as a war between the "Sons of Light" and the "Sons of Darkness." This tale refers to a Prince of Light, generally thought to be Michael, who leads the angelic ranks into battle. However, in this version of the war in Heaven, it is not Lucifer but Belial who leads the angelic rebellion. While a number of elements from this story resemble those from the Enochian and Judeo-Christian war in Heaven, they are not the same. Some see the Dead Sea Scrolls version of the "War between the Sons" as an entirely separate event. After all, there is nothing to support the idea that Lucifer was the first (or last) angel to try his hand at overthrowing the order of Heaven.

In the Christian biblical tradition, Michael is one of two angels identified by name (the other being Gabriel). What follows are a number of biblical passages that mention the archangel Michael. From the book of Daniel:

And at that time shall Michael stand up, the great prince who stands for the children of Thy people: and there shall be a time of trouble, such as never was since there was a nation even to that same time: and at that time Thy people shall be delivered, every one that shall be found written in the book.

—DANIEL 12:1

In the book of Joshua, Joshua encounters an angel who is generally believed to be the archangel Michael:

And it came to pass, when Joshua was by Jericho, that he lifted up his eyes and looked, and, behold, there stood a man over against him with his sword drawn in his hand: and Joshua went unto him, and said unto him, "Art thou for us, or for our adversaries?" And he said, "Nay; but as captain of the host of the Lord I now come." And Joshua fell on his face to the earth, and did worship, and said unto him, "What message does my Lord have for his servant?" And the captain of the Lord's host said unto Joshua, "Loose thy shoe from off thy foot; for the place thou stands is holy." And Joshua did so.

—JOSHUA 5:13–15

And, of course, there is a mention of Michael going toe-to-toe with Lucifer in Revelation (for more on Saint John's Revelation, see chapter 11):

And there was war in Heaven: Michael and his angels fought against the dragon; and the dragon fought alongside his own angels, and prevailed not; neither was a place for them found any longer in heaven. And the great dragon was cast out, that serpent of old, called the Devil, the Great Adversary, which deceives the whole world: he was cast out into the earth, and his angels were cast out with him. And I heard a loud voice saying in heaven, "Now comes salvation, and strength, and the kingdom of God, and the power of Christ: for the accuser of our brethren has been cast down, which accused them before our

God day and night. And they overcame him by the blood of the Lamb, and by the word of their testimony; and they loved not their lives unto the death. Therefore, rejoice ye Heavens, and ye that dwell in them. Woe to the inhabitants of the earth and sea! For the devil has come down unto you, having great wrath, because he knows that he hath but a short time."

—REVELATION 12: 1–12

Appropriately enough, the Catholic Prayer to Saint Michael the Archangel is considered one of the most powerful prayers of protection against demonic forces. There are a number of alternative versions of this prayer. The longest version is also the original, which was issued by order of the Roman Catholic Church's 257th leader, Pope Leo XIII, and meant for use as a protective prayer against demonic forces during exorcism rites.

There are three primary versions that are most commonly used by modern exorcists, mediums, and paranormal investigators. The shortest version has become the most frequently used, since it is easier to memorize. The short version of the prayer is as follows:

Saint Michael the Archangel, defend us in battle.
Be our protection against the wickedness and snares of the
    devil.
May God rebuke him, we humbly pray.
And do thou, Oh Prince of the Heavenly Host, by God's power,
    thrust into hell Satan and all evil spirits who wander the
    world seeking the ruin of souls.
Amen.

URIEL: HEAVENLY HIT MAN

Don't worry. I'll kill her gentle..

—URIEL, "HEAVEN AND HELL" (4-10)

In *Supernatural*, the archangel Uriel is portrayed as a kind of angelic hit man. Certainly, he is among the tougher of the archangels, almost on par with the likes of Michael. Uriel's name (sometimes spelled Oriel) means "light/fire of God" or "My light/fire is God." *Ur/Or* is a Hebrew word that can mean either "fire" or "light," while El is the proper Hebrew noun for referring to God.

While Uriel is one of the more commonly named archangels, his name does not appear in the Christian Bible. It does appear, however, in the book of Enoch. And the Uriel of the book of Enoch is a very high-ranking angel indeed, referred to as "leader of the All [the angels]." Some have interpreted this to mean that, at least at some point, Uriel might have outranked Michael in the angelic hierarchy. Maybe this is why he's so grumpy.

Though it is not directly stated in the television show, one could propose that the Uriel of *Supernatural* might have been demoted as a result of his blatant dislike for humans. After all, in *Supernatural* at least, Uriel does not seem to hold a much higher opinion of human beings than Lucifer does. In the episode "It's the Great Pumpkin, Sam Winchester" (4-7), Uriel speaks negatively in reference to humans on more than one occasion, calling them "mud monkeys," "savages," and "just plumbing on two legs." Castiel even scolds Uriel for using such derogatory language for humans, warning his fellow angel, "You're close to blasphemy."

In the book of Enoch, the archangel Uriel reveals to the scribe Enoch the secret workings of the planets and celestial bodies. Uriel's job is to keep the mysteries of existence, both deep within the depths of the Earth and beyond the known universe. At times this means protecting humankind from itself, by keeping humans from uncovering those things that might bring them harm—which would certainly include keeping them from opening old Lucifer's cage.

Of all the seven "Throne Angels," those angels who are allowed before the throne of God, Uriel is said to assume the closest position to it. As his name suggests, Uriel is closely associated with the sun. In ancient times, he was said to be the guardian of the "Great Light" (the sun) as it passed into the depths of darkness, which was then believed to exist below the visible Earth. Ancient cosmological traditions often believed that the evening sun descended into a dark underworld and thus required protection from the evil and violent entities that inhabited it. Uriel was likely seen as the angel tasked with defending the sun from harm until it completed its cycle and returned light to the world each dawn.

The idea that the sun descended into an evil realm of darkness most likely has its origins from the time of the ancient prophet Zoroaster, sometime between 1700 BCE and 1200 BCE, who portrayed the benevolent god Ahura Mazda as the protector of the sun during its nightly journey into the evil underworld of his rival, the malevolent god Angra Mainyu (for more on the Zoroastrian concept of Apocalypse, see chapter 9). In relation to Uriel's association with the solar cycle, he is said to be at his most powerful during the daylight (which must suck, considering that lore claims he spends every night fighting against demons in a dark underworld). Uriel supposedly exercises his greatest influence during the second hour of daylight.

ZACHARIAH: HEAVEN'S "DOUCHE-NOZZLE"

The end is nigh. The Apocalypse is coming, kiddo . . . to a theater near you.

—ZACHARIAH, "LUCIFER RISING" (4-22)

The angel Zachariah from *Supernatural* has many names, the choicest of which are usually given to him by Dean Winchester— "Chuckles," "Ass-hat," and the "Ghost of Christmas Screw You," to name just a few. However, like Castiel, there is not an angel in the Judeo-Christian tradition by the name of Zachariah. So, once again, discovering the mythological roots of the character requires a little detective work.

The answer to the root of the name Zachariah may be found in something called theophory, which refers to the linguistic differentiation in Hebrew between two nouns that are used to refer to God: El and Yah/Jah. Both words technically mean "God." However, the use of El is believed to originate from a more ancient Semitic tradition than does the use of Yah/Jah. There is an angel in the Judaic tradition named Zachari*el* (sometimes spelled Zechariel or Zacharael). The translation of this name has a number of possible interpretations, such as "El/God remembers" or "El/God has remembered" or "My memory is El/God." The meaning of the name can also be interpreted inversely: "remember(ing) El/God" or "My remembrance is of El/God."

If one were to exchange the El in the name Zachariel for Yah, the name becomes Zachariah. Interestingly enough, the switch from El to Yah does not change the meaning of the name whatsoever. Yah is simply a different noun with the same meaning, so Zachariah is "Yah/God remembers" instead of "El/God remembers."

There is the possibility that the name of the angel Zachariel evolved from an older name of one of the seven archangels named in the book of Enoch, Saraqael. It is possible that there were once two separate angels named Saraqael and Zachariel and that confusion arose owing to the phonetic similarities between their names. This may have eventually led the two angels to become integrated or mistakenly seen as one and the same entity. When researching either of these angels, one is likely to find that they are said to share a majority of attributes.

The meaning of the name Saraqael in the book of Enoch, however, is entirely different from that of Zachariel. Saraqael can be interpreted as meaning something like "God commands" or "God has commanded" or "My command is from God."

When it comes to the character Zachariah, however, it is more than likely that the creators of *Supernatural* were looking at the angel Zachariel (not Saraqael) when they created him. Zachariel is the patron angel of surrender. Traditionally, it is Zachariel's job to influence humans so that they will surrender to the will of God (whatever that may be). Of course, the Zachariah of *Supernatural* went rogue in the end and was no longer following God's will but instead claiming it as his own. Considering how diligently and vehemently Zachariah has worked at trying to convince Dean to accept his role as the human vessel of the archangel Michael, and how violently frustrated Zachariah becomes at Dean's constant refusals to say yes, it sort of makes sense. When you compare the two in this way, Zachariel begins to sound a lot like Zachariah. Both of them are all about getting humans to do what Heaven wants of them.

GABRIEL: IN ANGEL WITNESS PROTECTION

> Okay, okay. So I got wings . . . like Kotex.
>
> —GABRIEL, "HAMMER OF THE GODS" (5-19)

The archangel Gabriel first came onto the scene during season 2 of *Supernatural*, in the episode "Tall Tales." Of course, no one knew his real identity at that point. When Gabriel first showed up, he was living incognito as a pagan trickster god named Loki (for more on Loki, see chapter 9). Apparently Gabriel had abandoned his post as an archangel and taken up the identity of a trickster in his own personal version of angelic "witness protection."

Alongside the archangel Michael, Gabriel is one of the only two angels referred to by name in the Old Testament of the Christian Bible. The translation of his name is commonly interpreted to mean "My strength is from God." However, at times it is interpreted to mean "strength of God" or "hero of God."

In both the Muslim and Judeo-Christian traditions, the archangel Gabriel is said to be second in rank only to his big brother

Michael. This may be why, in season 5 of *Supernatural*, Gabriel believes he might be strong enough to take down Lucifer on his own in the "Hammer of the Gods" episode. After all, Gabriel is supposed to be one of the two most powerful angels in Heaven. If any angel other than Michael could take down "Luci," it'd probably be Gabriel. Of course, this reasoning turns out to be dead wrong when Lucifer shanks Gabriel in the chest with an angel sword.

Gabriel's role as an angel is often considered as something like the announcer, bugler, or trumpeter of Heaven. However, Gabriel is much more than just some mouthy angel who "blows a trumpet." His nature is far too complex for him to be typecast as such. This rather narrow portrayal has even led some to rather mistakenly consider Gabriel as the Judeo-Christian equivalent of the Greco-Roman messenger god Hermes/Mercury. Of course, anyone who saw the "Hammer of the Gods" episode knows that Gabriel and Mercury are portrayed as entirely different characters on the show. So it is probably safe to say that the creators of *Supernatural* did not adopt this particular stance.

In angelic lore, Gabriel acts as a divine messenger. In the Muslim tradition it is the archangel Gabriel who is credited with having brought the revelation of Islam to the prophet Muhammad. Muhammad is said to have recited the words of the Qur'an to a scribe after they were relayed to him by Gabriel. Because of this, the Muslim tradition considers Gabriel to be the patron angel of truth.

The Gabriel of *Supernatural* has a knack for reconstructing physical reality, or at least manipulating what humans see, hear, and even feel. I mean, we are talking about a guy who once made a frat boy believe he'd been abducted, probed by, and forced to slow dance with . . . wait for it . . . aliens. There are mythological portrayals of Gabriel that support this idea. For example, one story in the Qur'an tells of how the archangel Gabriel came down from Heaven on a holy steed when the Jews constructed the Golden Calf after their escape from Egypt (this would be the Muslim version of the Judeo-Christian story from the book of Exodus). In the story, Gabriel's holy steed threw up great clouds of dust in its wake. When some of this dust found its way into the mouth of the Golden Calf, it began to move and behave as if it were alive. The Golden Calf then went on a violent tear, showing the Jews the error of constructing a lifeless idol when the one and only living god was Allah.

The mythological Gabriel displays a very unique set of balanced yet seemingly contradicting characteristics and attributes. His various roles make him a sort of angelic representation of binary and dualistic behaviors. For starters, Gabriel is the patron angel of mercy as well as vengeance. He is not only the patron angel of death but also of resurrection (which definitely matches with the Gabriel in *Supernatural*, who once killed and resurrected Dean Winchester hundreds of times in a single episode). He is the angel of annunciation (meaning "to announce or tell" but not necessarily "show") but also an angel of revelation (which means "to show or reveal" but not necessarily "tell"). When one first considers these rather oppositional sounding roles, Gabriel seems to perform many tasks that would require him to possess contrary natures. Upon closer inspection, however, it becomes clear that Gabriel instead represents the natural order of existence, which exists as a balance of opposing forces. In mythological circles, Gabriel is sometimes considered a metaphorical representation of the divine balance that allows countless binary forces to assume a harmonious balance, which allows our physical reality to exist (without darkness, for example, there can be no light; without death, there can be no life).

RAPHAEL: HEALER AND DESTROYER

You got wasted by a Teenage Mutant Ninja Angel?

—DEAN WINCHESTER, "FREE TO BE YOU AND ME" (5-3)

Any fan of *Supernatural* is aware that Raphael is not the kind of archangel you want to mess with (then again, is there a kind of archangel that you *would* want to mess with?). When Castiel and Dean meet up with Raphael in an abandoned hovel, he shows up with wings of lightning and knocks out the electricity for the entire eastern seaboard. He is also responsible for smiting Castiel in the season 4 finale. Of course, this was not revealed until early in season 5 when Chuck delivered some of the show's most hilarious lines yet:

The archangel smote the crap out of him.

He like . . . exploded . . . like a water balloon full of chunky soup.

and

Oh, God. Is that a molar? I have a molar in my hair . . . It's
been a really stressful day.

—"SYMPATHY FOR THE DEVIL" (5-1)

The name of the archangel Raphael is usually interpreted
to mean "God has healed." Behind the archangels Michael and
Gabriel, Raphael is widely considered the third-highest ranking
angel in Heaven. As his name suggests, Raphael is widely considered an angel of healing and medicine, science and learning. However, one day his healing will come to an end and he will turn to
destruction as one of the Seven Angels of the Apocalypse.

Raphael is not mentioned by name in the Christian Bible.
However, he is named in a number of apocryphal texts, the oldest
being the book of Enoch. Raphael is also referred to by name in an
apocryphal text called the book of Tobit, the validity of which has
long been a matter of religious debate. The mention of Raphael's
name in the book of Tobit has led some to mistakenly believe that
Raphael is one of three angels named in the Bible. However, Raphael's name has not been among the biblically named angels since
the book of Tobit was removed from the Judeo-Christian canon.

In the book of Tobit, the archangel Raphael is responsible for
guiding and protecting Tobias, the son of Tobit (from whom the
text received its name), during his journey to the great ancient city
of Nineveh. In order to travel alongside Tobias without freaking
him out, Raphael assumes the guise of a normal human being. It
is not until Tobias reaches Nineveh that Raphael reveals his true
form and "uncases his wings." Raphael then explains to Tobias
that he is one of the Seven Holy Angels that are allowed to stand
or kneel before God's throne.

Like his brother Gabriel, Raphael has a varied nature and is known by a number of titles and roles. Many of his roles, as in the book of Tobit, involve protecting people and places. Raphael is known by the title "Protector of the Eden Tree," because after God's expulsion of Adam and Eve for eating the forbidden fruit of the Eden Tree he was tasked with guarding the tree, while outside his fellow cherubim guarded the gates. He is also the Guardian of the Western Horizon. His heavenly role is Prince of the Second Level of Heaven. In some of the more recent Judeo-Christian traditions, Raphael is considered the angel of happiness, light, love, and prayer. He also belongs to the angelic orders of both the cherubim and seraphim.

Even before Raphael was introduced on the show, his name had already been mentioned on at least one occasion. In season 2, episode 13, "Houses of the Holy," a priest named Father Reynolds performs last rites for the wayward spirit of a fellow priest named Father Gregory, in order to send his spirit to the "other side." As he is reciting the last rites, Father Reynolds says, "I call upon the archangel Raphael, angel of the air."

This invocation of Raphael is not a part of the standard, authorized last rites that are used by priests of the Roman Catholic Church. In fact, it comes from a lesser-known version of last rites that is used by a priestly order known as the Holy Order of Mans. This order is no longer endorsed by the Roman Catholic Church, but it is believed that many members of the priesthood remain members in secret to an order called the Christ the Savior Brotherhood.

Here is an excerpt from the last rites of the Holy Order of Mans, which were recited by Father Reynolds in the "Houses of the Holy" episode:

Oh Holy Hosts above, I call upon thee as a servant of Jesus Christ, to sanctify our actions this day in preparation for the fulfillment of the will of God. I call upon the great archangel Raphael, Master of Air, to open the way for this to be done. Let the fire of the Holy Spirit now descend that this being might be awakened to the world beyond and the life of the earth, and infused with the power of the Holy Spirit. Oh Lord Jesus Christ, most merciful, Lord of Earth we ask that you receive this child into your arms, that he might pass in safety from this crisis.

ANNA MILTON: RAGUEL OR REMIEL?

Anna Milton is a powerful angel who chose to rip out her grace, fall to the Earth, and become mortal. While her angelic name is never clearly identified, the creators of the show do offer some clues. We already know that when she was an angel, Anna was the boss of many of the angels, including Zachariah and Uriel. Needless to say, this would mean she was very powerful. Anna also claims that she and Uriel "shared the same foxhole," which would suggest that she was once an archangel. Since Michael, Raphael, Gabriel, Uriel, and Saraqael (Zachariah) have already been identified, there are only two options left: Raguel or Remiel.

Given how powerful Anna is after she regains her lost grace, it is more than likely that she is the vengeful archangel Raguel instead of Remiel. Raguel would have been on the front lines during

---

SUPERNATURAL FACTS

Anna Milton may or may not be the archangel Raguel or Remiel. However, it is more than likely that her last name, Milton, was chosen as a reference to seventeenth-century English poet John Milton. Milton penned a well-known poem titled *Paradise Lost*, which concerns the history of humanity's fall from grace. Considering Anna's more literal "fall," after tearing out her own "grace," the last name Milton seems more than fitting.

---

the war in Heaven, which would explain the various sorts of battlefield references that Anna Milton makes on the show.

"CUPID" AND THE CHERUBIM

In season 5, episode 14, "My Bloody Valentine," Sam, Dean, and Castiel come face-to-face with a cherub named Cupid. In mythology, Cupid is the name of a Greco-Roman god of love, not an angel, and in the Judeo-Christian tradition the cherubim have nothing to do with human matchmaking. However, there have long been artistic portrayals of cherubim as bow-wielding, youthful (almost infantile) winged beings. Cupid is also often portrayed with wings and a quiver of arrows, so it is likely the creators of *Supernatural* simply decided to integrate the two traditions.

In the Judeo-Christian tradition, cherubim are the winged angels tasked with both holding up the throne of God and acting as guardian angels for humans. In Ezekiel the cherubim are said to carry around the chariot of God (which also held God's throne). In relation to the angelic order of the seraphim, cherubim are ranked under them as the second-highest order of angels.

SUPERNATURAL FACTS

The strange, somewhat heart-shaped symbol that Dean and Sam discover etched into the actual hearts of the Horseman of Famine's first victims (who, grossly enough, ate each other to death) is the Enochian magic sign for the word *nach*, which sounds like "knock" but with more phlegm at the end. When Castiel uses an Enochian incantation to summon Cupid in the back of the restaurant, you can hear him say this word.

When Adam and Eve were booted out, and the gates became closed forever under the guard of Raphael, the cherubim were the guardians of the Garden of Eden. Before this, it is likely that the cherubim protected Adam and Eve from the dangerous world outside of Eden's protection. As it is written in Genesis 3:24: "So God drove out Man; and he placed the cherubim at the east side of Eden, and a flaming sword which turned in all directions, to bar the way to the tree of life."

The cherubim are referred to again in Exodus 25:18–20, in which it is written, "They [the cherubim] were placed at the Garden's gates to prevent humans from returning and gaining access to the Tree of Life. They also formed the seat of mercy on the Ark of the Covenant."

WHEN ANGELS GO BAD

So, what happens when angels go rogue? Well, God usually shows up, amps up the loyal angels with superpowers, and has them smite the crap out of the rogue angels. If you need proof, just look at what happened to Lucifer and Azazel. So why hasn't God shown up and done this yet in *Supernatural*? Why haven't the angels who kick-started the Apocalypse been sent to rot alongside Lucifer? All this chaos, and God has done nothing to the rogue angels . . . or has he?

When you think about it, justice has been served to a point. Zachariah got skewered by Dean wielding Castiel's angel sword. Michael fell into the pit with his brother Lucifer (both of whom, unfortunately, were still wearing Adam and Sam as meat suits), just in time for Dean to reseal it. So, in a sense, Zachariah and Michael have both been made to suffer. Even Uriel got his just desserts. Was this a way for the writers of *Supernatural* to suggest God's involvement? Of course, now that Sam is back out of the pit, and finally has his soul back . . . only time will tell.

$\Longequal 5 \Longequal$

LIKE A BAT OUT OF HELL

What is it with you Winchesters? You . . . your dad. You're both just itchin' to throw yourselves down in the pit.
—BOBBY SINGER, "ALL HELL BREAKS LOOSE: PART 2" (2-22)

One doesn't have to watch *Supernatural* very long to become aware that all three of the Winchester boys tend to die a lot—especially Dean. In one episode alone, it is suggested that Dean Winchester dies well over a hundred times (though we are only allowed to see him killed on about a dozen of those occasions). Bearing all this in mind, perhaps it should be no surprise that the Winchesters have a rather intimate relationship with the afterlife—Heaven and Hell and everything in between.

HEAVEN ABOVE, HELL BELOW

The belief in some form of "Heaven above" and "Hell below" has existed in human mythological traditions since ancient times, and the concept is surprisingly universal. For example, the ancient Norse believed in a heavenly Valhalla, as well as a dark underworld ruled over by the goddess Hel.

Even in *Supernatural*, Heaven and Hell are portrayed as existing in reference to vertical directions; Heaven is thought of as being "up there," and Hell is said to be "down there." However, upon more detailed consideration, most people would not agree with the idea that Heaven truly exists somewhere in the sky or that Hell can literally be located in some subterranean location. So why do we humans still tend to look up to the skies when we think of Heaven and think of Hell as someplace below our feet? The answers to these questions likely lie in the earliest human understandings about life and death.

The skies above were, in ancient times, considered an eternally unreachable place. In the same way, what lay beneath the Earth was a mysterious and dark place into which humans feared to venture. Both places represented great mysteries to the human mind and were therefore associated with the ever-greater mysteries of the divine and the afterlife. Only gods could ascend to the skies, and only devils could exist in the dark below.

When someone died, the ancient mind must have reasoned that the body would begin to rot and so had to be buried in the Earth or in some other way disposed of properly. Perhaps the metaphorical concept of Hell as a place within the Earth was a subconscious human acknowledgment that our bodily desires and physical limitations were preventing our souls from transcending, that is, ascending to Heaven. To reach Heaven, one had to forever vacate one's physical body and transcend physical reality. Therefore, one had to escape Earth itself, which, it may have been reasoned, meant going up into the unknown realms of skies above.

One interesting element to the mythology of Heaven and Hell is that one is seen as absolute while the other is, well, not exactly absolute. Often, a heavenly reward is considered permanent. For example, one rarely hears mythological tales of humans (not angels, mind you) who initially dwelled in Heaven only to be later thrown down into Hell. However, there are tales of souls who find salvation and are allowed to ascend to Heaven, or at least to some less terrible plane of existence, after being cast into the pit of Hell. In fact, this idea plays a large role in Christian (especially Catholic) mythology, in the story of Christ's Harrowing of Hell, which is laid out in lines 4 to 6 in the Apostles' Creed of the Roman Catholic Church:

Line 4: He suffered under Pontius Pilate, was crucified, died, and was entombed.

Line 5: He descended into hell, and on the third day he rose.

Line 6: He then ascended to Heaven and sits at the right hand of the Father.

Similar versions of this creed exist in the Anglican, Lutheran, United Methodist, and Presbyterian churches. The creed does not specify the reason Christ went into Hell or the tasks he performed while there. In Catholicism, however, it is believed that Christ descended to Hell in order to liberate the souls of some who died before his coming. Many of those said to have been rescued during Christ's Harrowing of Hell are specified in Dante Alighieri's poem *Purgatorio* (his better-known poem, *Inferno*, will be discussed in the next section). They include Greek philosophers, such as Socrates and Plato, whose teachings had become central to the education of the clergy. This mythological idea was mainly introduced in order to give some sort of justification for the church's authorization and endorsement of works written by pagans, who, according to their dogma, would have to be in Hell.

The narrow dogmatic view that only those non-Christians included in the Harrowing of Hell story can enter Heaven is not, of course, endorsed by *Supernatural*. In "Dark Side of the Moon" (5-16), Ash explains to the Winchester brothers that he has met Vatsyayana, the author of the Kama Sutra, and who is most definitely a Hindu, during his time in Heaven. So it would seem that religious affiliation, as far as the *Supernatural* mythos is concerned, has zero effect on whether or not a person is allowed a place in Heaven.

When Dean Winchester is pulled from the pit by Castiel, it follows along with this mythological tradition that only by some divine force could a person become freed from Hell. However, not every Winchester needed the help of an angel to get out of the fiery depths. When a Devil's Gate, a portal between Hell and Earth, is temporarily opened in Wyoming (of all places) by one of the yellow-eyed demon's "special children" in "All Hell Breaks Loose:

Part 2," John Winchester manages to claw his way out of the pit on his own.

One of the fairly new ideas concerning the concept of Hell has to do with its relation to time. It is said that human time crawls in comparison to "Hell time." For example, Dean Winchester's seemingly brief three-month stint in the pit was actually more like forty years as time passes in Hell. John Winchester suffered in that horrible place for just short of one human year, or roughly one hundred "Hell years." Similar portrayals of this idea have occurred in such films as the 2005 movie *Constantine*, in which time is shown to stop when the boundary between Hell and Earth is crossed. The main character of the film states: "Take it from me, two minutes in Hell is a lifetime."

HELL ACCORDING TO DANTE

While the Hell mythology used by the creators of *Supernatural* is not specifically named, there are clues that would suggest that certain elements have been adopted from medieval Italian poet Dante Alighieri's *Inferno*. While in Latin the term *inferno* literally means an out-of-control fire, in Italian it is used in reference to Hell. This work is the first part of a three-part collection titled *La Divina Commedia* (or The Divine Comedy), the next two sections being *Purgatorio* (Purgatory, also known as Limbo) and *Paradiso* (Paradise, or Heaven).

Dante's tale begins on the day preceding Good Friday in the year 1300, when the narrator (Dante himself) is thirty-five years old. While Dante's true date of birth is unknown, many scholars use the poem as a reference point, and so it is commonly believed that he was born sometime in May or June of 1265. Though the tale is meant to be considered allegorical instead of literal, at the time there were many in the church who viewed it as a divine revelation.

In the story, Dante awakens in a "Dark Wood" and finds himself face-to-face with the ancient Roman poet Virgil. From this dark and morbid forest the pair embarks on a detailed tour of the various levels of Hell. In Dante's mythology, the entrance to Hell is found at the edge of the Dark Wood, beyond which is an outer area, "the Vestibule," in which are punished the Opportunists, meaning those who were neither good nor evil in their lives but instead selfishly chose only to do that which was most beneficial to them. These souls are forced to forever chase an unreachable banner (a symbol of "choosing a side"), on a ground covered by maggots, all the while being themselves chased by hordes of stinging hornets. These people were not evil, so they do not deserve the extreme punishments of Hell. However, they were not good people, either, and so have not earned their places in Heaven. Dante claims that an afterlife in the Vestibule is the ultimate price of a life of indifference.

At the edge of the Vestibule is the river Acheron. There Dante and Virgil are given passage across by the ferryman Charon, an obvious reference to the Greek mythological ferryman Charon who ferried souls across the river Styx to the underworld realm of the god Hades. Once across the river Acheron, Dante is introduced to nine specific levels of Hell. These levels are usually depicted in one of two ways. The first way is one-dimensional, depicted as concentric circles that move inward (basically, the deeper into Hell Dante goes, the smaller the circle becomes). However, the more popular depiction is three-dimensional, showing the levels as sections of an ever-narrowing cone, with the wide lip being Limbo and the deepest level of Hell being the tip. The levels of Dante's Hell are as follows:

LEVEL 1—LIMBO: Limbo, or Purgatory, is reserved for "virtuous pagans" (such as Virgil), many of whom were brought there during Christ's Harrowing of Hell. Dante claims this is where good people who were not Christians end up. And Limbo is not all that bad, to be honest. No terrible punishments are reserved for those who dwell here. However, there are no heavenly rewards, either. While this certainly would not be the kind of tormented existence common of the devil's pit, you have to admit that it sounds really, *really* boring. Imagine having to spend eternity just sitting around, staring at the walls (would Limbo even have walls?), and you have a good idea what it would be like in this first level of Hell.

> Purgatory is vast, underutilized, and Hell adjacent . . . and I want it.
>
> —CROWLEY, "FAMILY MATTERS" (6-7)

As already stated, Purgatory is a realm of the afterlife that is reserved for those individuals who were neither entirely good nor evil during their lives. In the episode "Family Matters" (6-7), we learn that this realm (according to the mythos of *Supernatural*) is also where the souls of monsters go when they die. This would seem to go against the natural conclusion that monsters would go to Hell. However, upon further consideration, Purgatory is a much more fitting destination for the souls of the monstrous. After all, monsters cannot help but be what they are. In their minds, they are not evil; they are just trying to survive. Vampires will die if they do not feed on blood, just as a lion will die if it does not feed on the gazelle. And, like the lion, the vampire would have no choice. By this rationale, Hell would be neither a just nor appropriate final destination for the souls of monsters. Monsters are evil, certainly, from the mortal human point of view. However, it is their inherent natures that make them so.

LEVEL 2—THE LUSTFUL: This is the first real "punishment" level of Hell. The inhabitants of this level are condemned to an eternity of being thrashed about and torn apart by a terrible and unceasing storm.

LEVEL 3—THE GLUTTONOUS: Those condemned to this level are trapped up to their torsos in rotting, putrid, stinking soil, which symbolizes how their lives were wasted on overindulgence. They are allowed neither to eat nor drink, and under the weight of the nasty soil, they are rendered helpless as the three-headed beast of legend, the dark hound called Cerberus (yet another reference to Greek mythology), tears them to pieces over and over.

LEVEL 4—THE WASTEFUL AND GREEDY: This section of Hell is reserved for those who wasted their resources on unnecessary frivolities as well as for those who hoarded their possessions or gave no alms to the poor despite having the means. The punishment in this level is rather weird. The Hoarders and the Wasters are set against one another in an eternal jousting match. However, the jousters are forced to use ridiculously heavy weights instead of lances. The Hoarders charge at the Wasters with the battle cry "Why do you waste?" and the Wasters charge the Hoarders with "Why do you hoard?"

LEVEL 5—THE TOWER OF STYX: The fifth level is surrounded by the boiling waters of the river Styx (yet another reference to Greek and Roman mythology). Here, the Wrathful, that is, the quick-tempered, vengeful, and unforgiving, swim the surface of the scalding waters of the Styx, forever fighting one another. Below the terrible waters are trapped the Sullen, people who unnecessarily feel sorry for themselves and enjoy selfishly evoking pity from others.

THE WALLS OF DIS: If Hell is a prison, then the levels up to this point have held the "light offenders." Beyond these walls lies the "City of Dis," which contains the deepest levels of Hell. These levels house the worst of Hell's inhabitants. The walls of Dis are guarded by the Three Furies and the Gorgon Medusa. In Greek and Roman mythology, the Furies were winged and wrathful female demigods who worked as the agents of divine justice. When the gods wished to punish an injustice, they sent the Furies. Medusa was a cursed, snake-haired, serpentlike female figure, capable of turning even half-god heroes and Titans to stone with no more than a look. These frightening figures attempt to bar Dante and Virgil from entering and threaten to do the poets harm until an angel arrives in order to secure their passage into the City of Dis.

LEVEL 6—HERETICS: Now, this is the Hell that most of us know! In this level, each of the condemned is encased in his or her own flaming sarcophagus. They suffer the constant and terrible pains of being burned alive, yet they are never allowed to die, and their bodies do not burn away.

LEVEL 7—THE THREE VIOLENT SINS: This section of Hell is broken up into specific subsections, based on three kinds of violence:

1. **River Phlegethon—Violence against Community:** A boiling river of blood known as Phlegethon is home to those who committed acts of violence against their neighbors and communities and acts of vandalism.

2. **Wood of Suicides—Violence against Self:** Those who took their own lives, committing violence against themselves, are condemned to the Wood of Suicides, where they are forced to assume the inanimate form of trees. In this unmovable state they are constantly torn apart by Harpies, birdlike creatures with the shrieking heads of women from Greek myth. Some inhabitants are allowed to keep their bodies, namely those who died as a result of their own foolish actions instead of by an act of deliberate suicide, but they are chased about the woods and repeatedly ripped apart by vicious black dogs.

3. **The Burning Sands—Violence against God or the Natural Order:** This desert, in which fire rains gently down from the sky like snowflakes, is for blasphemers, sexual perverts, and

rapists. It is also where usurers (not to be confused with usurpers) are kept. Usurers are loan-givers who charge unfair interest.

LEVEL 8—MALEBOLGE, "THE TERRIBLE DITCH": This is one of the scariest levels of Hell, and like level 7 it is broken up into various subsections. However, to go into detail about each would take up multiple chapters. To give a basic rundown, this terrible level of Hell is reserved for the following types of offenders:

Panderers and Seducers: People who begged for money despite being able to work or who used other dishonest means to obtain money are considered panderers and seducers. In the modern vernacular, we would say con artists, pimps, prostitutes, and gold diggers.

Sycophants and Flatterers: These are individuals who, during life, gave insincere flattery in order to gain status or favor.

Sorcerers and False Prophets: This refers to those who use dark magic (or pretend to be able to do so) for personal gain as well as to those who falsely claim to have been granted divine knowledge.

Bribers and Simoniacs: In Dante's time, this specifically referred to those who practiced simony, the buying of high-ranking religious offices. A modern equivalent of simony might be lobbyists who bribe politicians for political favors.

Extortionists and Power Abusers: These individuals misuse power or use their authority for personal gain.

Hypocrites: These are people who don't do as they tell others to do or who criticize others for doing things they do themselves.

Thieves: These are people who made their livings by theft.

False Advisers: This refers to those who intentionally give false counsel or do so under false credentials.

Sowers of Discord: People who incite chaos and hostility and who bring about wars for personal gain fall into this category.

Falsifiers and Counterfeiters: For Dante, this would have referred mainly to those who created false documents.

LEVEL 9—COCYTUS: This final level of Hell is reserved for traitors. This section consists almost entirely of ice and is encircled by giants and Titans (integrating both biblical and Greek myths) who are trapped in it. Since this level of Hell is for betrayers, perhaps it is only fitting that this is where the fallen angel Lucifer, the big cheese of Hell himself, is kept trapped. In the center of Cocytus, the Prince of Lies stands encased in solid ice up to his chest (so, yes, it would seem Hell *has* frozen over). Among those keeping Lucifer company in Cocytus are Judas, who betrayed Christ, and Brutus, who conspired to assassinate Julius Caesar.

Based on what we have seen and heard about his time in Hell, it would appear that Dean Winchester was subjected to several different tortures found in the sublevels of the pit of Malebolge. For example, at the end of the season 3 finale, "No Rest for the

Wicked," we are shown Dean being suspended from flesh hooks over a fiery sea of red and black.

In the parts of Malebolge reserved for the corrupt and extortionists, souls are strung up by demons using flesh hooks and suspended over boiling cauldrons of black tar. In the *bolge* (pit) that is specially reserved for Sowers of Discord, a blade-wielding demon slices his victims to ribbons over and over again. Alastair, the demon who tortured Dean in Hell by flaying him alive every day, is often referred to as "Picasso with a razor." Perhaps Alastair is a Malebranche, a demon of Malebolge, or even the Malacoda (leader of the Malebranche) incarnate.

Alastair is also referred to by the title of Hell's chief torturer, which would certainly match up with the role of Dante's Malacoda. As explained in chapter 3, there is no known demon in mythology that goes by the name Alastair. However, under the pretense of allowing Dante and Virgil safe passage, Malacoda deceives the two men, and for a time he and his Malebranche chase and threaten them within the fifth pit of Malebolge. This combination of malice, torture, and deception certainly seems to describe Alastair.

Of the forty or so Hell years that Dean Winchester spent down in the pit, he was tormented by Alastair for only thirty of them. Every day, Dean would be sliced to pieces by Alastair only to be regenerated so that he could suffer the whole ordeal again. And each day his demonic tormenter would offer him the same deal. If Dean would only agree to take up a blade and torture other souls (perhaps to become one of the Malebranche?), then he would cease to be tortured. But every man has a breaking point, and Dean's was thirty years. For the next ten Hell years, Dean joined Alastair and actively tortured other damned souls. After a time, Dean later confessed to Sam, he even grew to like it. Who knows how close Dean came to becoming a demon himself?

THE SACRIFICE PARADOX

Mythical tradition states that any person who trades his or her soul to the devil is doomed to suffer in Hell for all eternity. However, Christian belief also states that sacrificing oneself for another is the most righteous act any human can perform. In fact, Jesus states in John 15:13, "There is no greater love than to lay down one's life for a friend." Taking both of these into consideration, a conflict arises.

What if one sacrifices one's life and soul in order to save someone else's, as John and Dean Winchester have done? According to the mythos surrounding Hell, making a deal with the devil (or crossroads demon) leads to damnation. Then again, this idea seems to contradict the universally held Christian belief in the righteousness of sacrifice. In *Supernatural*, a deal with a crossroads demon (regardless of your reasons for making it) is seen as a binding contract that cannot be broken, and you must submit to Hell's wrath once your contract's allotted time has expired.

Supernatural is not the only work in recent years to address this scenario of selling one's soul to save another. In the 2005 film *Constantine*, starring Keanu Reeves and based on the comic book series *Hellblazer*, the protagonist escapes Hell's clutches by making a deal with Lucifer that would trade his own soul for a young woman who committed suicide to avoid being possessed. Lucifer agrees to the deal but then finds himself unable to collect as Constantine is torn from his grip by an unseen divine force.

WHERE IN THE HELL IS HELL, ANYWAY?

Over the many millennia of human existence, there have probably existed just as many ideas about exactly where Hell is located. Modern belief usually considers Hell, if it is believed to even be a place, as a nonphysical dimension that exists separately from and/ or overlapping with our own. Some believe that Hell is a metaphor for the suffering caused by existing in our physical three-dimensional reality. Some myths have said that Hell is a place in the depths of the Earth. Some religious traditions have even claimed that Hell is located in the sun (though this idea has long been dismissed). The truth of the matter is . . . who in the hell knows where to find Hell?

In *Supernatural*, the barrier between Hell and Earth is a pretty flimsy one. The only thing keeping nearly every last member of the legions of Hell . . . well, in Hell where they belong . . . is a series of rare portals called Devil's Gates. When these portals are opened, it's every demon for itself. It is generally agreed that demons prefer torturing the living far more than they do the damned. And when this happens, it often results in cases of demonic possession.

The idea of a real-life Devil's Gate might seem far-fetched. However, in recent centuries thousands of people have bought into (some quite literally) a fictitious account of one such gate. In fact, it stands as one of the most widespread religious-centered urban legends of modern times.

The story usually goes something like this:

While performing deep drilling in a remote location in Russia (usually Siberia), a drill crew began to experience increasingly strange phenomena. Upon reaching an extreme depth, the drill bit began to rotate unusually quickly as if it had hit a hollow section. Soon, the instruments began to give strange temperature readings of roughly 2,000 degrees Fahrenheit. The bit was then removed and a probe was sent down into the pipe in order to record information. The recording device on the probe was said to have recorded the sounds of terrible screams and demonic laughter. The drilling crew, it seemed, had drilled into Hell itself.

Most people know this story as the "Drilling to Hell" incident. The story first gained widespread acceptance, especially among the conservative Christian community, when it was televised by the Trinity Broadcast Network (TBN) during the late 1980s and early '90s. Many investigators, skeptics and believers alike, of the purported incident called into the station asking for details. Station representatives always claimed to have "irrefutable evidence" to prove the story's validity.

The irrefutable evidence, however, was a little sketchy. According to TBN, which published the account repeatedly in its newsletter, the story was translated from an article found in a Finnish newspaper called *Ammennusatia*. The TBN station, however, did not receive the article directly from the source. It originally received the story from a Texas evangelist named R. W. Schambach, a regular guest and lecturer on the network's programs. However, even Schambach had not received the article directly from *Ammennusatia*. He had received the story from a Norwegian man named Age Rendalen, who had written a letter of confirmation supporting the validity of the story to Schambach. According to Rendalen, reports about the incident were all over Finland. Along with the letter, Rendalen included what he claimed to be a translation of the original *Ammennusatia* article. He also assured Schambach and TBN that *Ammennusatia* was one of Finland's most reputable newspapers as well as a notable scientific journal. Rendalen also claimed to have gone to the site himself and included details about witnessing a winged creature rise up out of the hole and escape from the drill site (presumably a demon).

When skeptics and journalists began looking into this, as will eventually happen in such cases, the story began to fall apart. As it turned out, *Ammennusatia* was most definitely *not* a respected newspaper—and certainly not a scientific journal. In fact, *Ammennusatia* was just a monthly newsletter published by Finnish Christian groups. The story published in *Ammennusatia* had actually been a secondhand account written by a staff member who claimed to have read it in an article published in *Etela-Suomen*, which is a real Finnish newspaper.

So now investigators began ringing the phones at *Etela-Suomen*, trying to find the root of the news story. It turned out to be a good news–bad news situation. The good news was that the story had, in fact, appeared in the Finnish paper. The bad news was that it hadn't been a news article. The story had been published in an op-ed section of the paper, in which the public could send in letters about whatever they wished.

A small number of skeptics and investigators (basically, those who hadn't given up on it) tried to track down the man who had originally sent in the story to *Etela-Suomen*. The gentleman was now in the later years of his life. The funny thing was that he told investigators that he had come across the story while reading a publication called *Vaeltajat*—a newsletter published by a Finnish Christian missionary group. And the search for the story's true origins continued.

When the investigators got in touch with *Vaeltajat*, they learned that the story had appeared in the July 1989 issue of the newsletter. The editor of *Vaeltajat* claimed that the story was sent in from one of its readers, who claimed to have read it in a U.S. publication called *Jewels of Jericho*, which was supposedly published by a group of Messianic Jews in California.

So the story had been spread in the United States under the pretense that it came from a source in Finland and had been published in Finland by a newsletter that believed it had gotten the story form a source in the States.

And the search continued.

But what about Rendalen, the Norwegian man who wrote letters to Schambach and TBN, who claimed to have been to the site himself? When investigators caught up with Rendalen, he finally came clean about the whole thing.

Rendalen explained that while on a trip to the United States he had seen a TBN broadcast about the so-called Drilling to Hell incident. He had been absolutely dumbfounded by the idea that anyone could believe such a thing. So, when he got back home to

Norway he decided to play a little gag on Schambach and the folks at TBN. He wrote the letters about his experience seeing the winged creature emerge from the hole. Along with his letter, he included his name, address, and telephone number as well as the contact information of a pastor he knew who lived in California. He also included his "translation," along with a Finnish article that he claimed to be the original.

Rendalen had figured that any fool who was willing to do even a little investigating would be able to figure out the story was a hoax in a heartbeat. Both Rendalen and his pastor friend had even resolved that they would tell the truth if anyone from TBN or Schambach's office contacted either one of them. They did not. In fact, it seems that neither of the groups so much as checked out a single detail of the story, not even the translation. The original "article" that Rendalen had included was actually a piece from his own local paper that had nothing to do with the story he claimed it was about. Apparently, no one had even bothered to check the accuracy of the translation. And yet they ran the story for years—and a staggering number of independent Christian newsletters continue to publish it despite the fact that an account of this entire chain of events (regarding the truth behind the story) was even published in a fairly reputable scholarly magazine, the *Biblical Archaeology Review*.

Many believers have sadly been duped by the scams of religious con artists looking to cash in on the hoax. In 1990 at least one skeptic investigator was contacted by an Arizona pastor who claimed that one of his parishioners had shown him proof that the Drilling to Hell incident was real. The parishioner claimed to have a PhD in physics from MIT and had explained to the pastor and his congregation how he had been a member of a secret scientific research team that had spent a year collecting data from the "Hell hole" site. He claimed that the microphones used to record sounds in the hole were continually being melted by the extreme heat. They had succeeded in recording only seventeen seconds at a time. According to the parishioner, the scientific team was about to reassemble once more in order to bring back conclusive proof of the existence of Hell. He also claimed that his role would be crucial, as he had designed a cooling system for the microphone that could withstand the 2,000 degree Fahrenheit temperature. However, he did not have the funding to make the return trip, so the congregation was planning to help him raise the funds.

Of course, just about everything the parishioner had told the pastor and his congregation later turned out to be a lie. He did not have a PhD in physics (or anything else, for that matter), and MIT had never heard of him. The man had never been a scientist, let alone a member of any secret scientific research team. The only thing the man had done was take off with the roughly twenty thousand dollars in funds that the congregation had raised for what was supposed to be his return trip to Siberia. Once the guy had his money, he bailed town and neither the pastor nor his congregation ever heard from him again.

Perhaps Dean Winchester said it best: "There's some legends you just file under 'bull-crap.'"

= 6 =

BEYOND THE GATES OF HEAVEN

This ain't the first time you've been here. I mean, you boys
die more than anyone I've ever met.

—ASH (AKA "DR. BADASS"), "DARK SIDE OF THE MOON" (5-16)

As already stated in the previous chapter, the Winchester
boys have made quite a few trips into the afterlife—both
Heaven and Hell. Of course, Sam and Dean don't know
this because the angels have "Windexed their brains." It is not
until the abovementioned episode, when they go to Heaven after
being killed by a couple of misguided hunters who believe that
Sam is some kind of Hell spawn, that the boys are allowed to remember their little side trip upstairs.

Aside from being the first episode to feature the character Ash
since his death near the end of season 2, this is the only *Supernatural* episode to offer a glimpse into the more pleasant "flip
side" of the afterlife—Heaven.

133

STAIRWAYS TO HEAVEN

CASTIEL: What do you see?

DEAN: What? Nothing!

CASTIEL: Some people see a tunnel or a river . . . what do you see?

DEAN: Nothing, my dash. I'm in my car; I'm on the road.

CASTIEL: All right . . . a road. For you, it's a road.

—DEAN WINCHESTER AND CASTIEL,
"DARK SIDE OF THE MOON" (5-16)

Mythology is littered with different paths meant to lead a soul to the afterlife or Heaven. This is especially true of ancient or "primal" myths. Primal myths are those that attempt to explain the creation of the world and humankind. In one African myth, for example, Heaven and Earth were once connected by a ladder or rope. Horrified at the violence of humans, however, the gods eventually decided to cut the rope and leave us to our own devices. But this is not the end of such symbolism. Different thresholds between Heaven and Earth can be found across the mythological spectrum.

Here are some additional examples of these mythical "stairways to Heaven":

- In Greek myth, one had to travel over the river Titan Oceanus to reach heavenly Elysium.

- In one myth of the Pacific Northwest Tlingit tribe, a hero

SUPERNATURAL FACTS

When Sam and Dean met up with Ash in his heavenly abode, a reconstruction of his beloved roadhouse where he used to sleep on the pool table, he mentioned that he had finally found a "practical application for string theory." Basically, this is a developing theory in quantum physics that claims that subatomic particles exist as one-dimensional "strings," each vibrating at its own unique frequency. Therefore, Ash is (more or less) able to differentiate between, and zero in on, different angels and/or souls in Heaven by identifying the unique frequencies of their "strings."

ascends to Heaven by shooting arrows into various celestial bodies and jumping from one to the next.

- In Roman Catholic lore, one must meet Saint Peter (said to have been given the keys to Heaven when he became the first pope) at the gates of Heaven, often called the pearly gates, in order to gain entrance.

- The Mayans believed that a there was rope that souls climbed to gain access to a sort of "road to Heaven."

- In Norse myths there was a bridge like a "burning rainbow" called Bifröst that connected the human realm (Midgard) with the realm of the gods (Asgard).

- In Hawaiian myths, there is a "road to Hana" (road to Heaven).

- In Judeo-Christian lore, Jacob, son of Isaac, ascended to Heaven by way of a ladder (hence the term *Jacob's ladder*).

- In Chinese folklore, it is said beings once traveled freely between Heaven and Earth by using a ladder.

There are all these ladders, roads, bridges, and tunnels—and yet not a single "Stairway to Heaven." Dean Winchester would be disappointed.

MY BLUE HEAVEN

See, you gotta stop thinking about Heaven as one place. It's more like *a butt-load* of places, all crammed together . . . like Disneyland, except without all the anti-Semitism.

—ASH, "DARK SIDE OF THE MOON" (5-16)

These days, you don't see many portrayals of the old "pearly towers, clouds, and harps" stereotype of Heaven. This shift in view most likely stems from the fact that humans have stopped thinking of Heaven as some place "up there." Considering that humans have walked on the moon, well beyond the clouds of the lower atmosphere that once commonly saturated portrayals of Heaven, perhaps this shouldn't be much of a surprise.

Since few can claim to have seen Heaven and lived, and since those who claim to have done so can't exactly prove it, just about everyone on the planet has a different idea as to exactly what

"Heaven" is. However, *Supernatural*'s portrayal of Heaven seems to be in keeping with an increasingly popular point of view—that Heaven is whatever someone wants it to be. At first it is simply a replay of one's "greatest hits," as Sam puts it. However, as time goes on, it would seem that individual souls are able to create their own "personal Heavens" that suit their particular views when it comes to eternal bliss and perfect happiness. After all, isn't that what Heaven is supposed to be all about?

SUPERNATURAL FACTS

As with many other *Supernatural* episodes, the title of "Dark Side of the Moon" comes from classic rock. *Dark Side of the Moon* was the title of an extremely successful album by the progressive rock group Pink Floyd, released in 1973.

Ash's Heaven, for example, is Harvelle's Roadhouse. As Dean points out, "It even smells the same," to which Ash replies, "Bud, blood, and beer nuts . . . Best smell in the world." For Ash, an eternity in the roadhouse (with an occasional "field trip" here and there, of course) is Heaven. Pamela (who gets her eyes back in Heaven, after having them burned out during her first encounter with Castiel) describes her Heaven to Dean as "one long show at the Meadowlands." You have to admit, it sounds like a pretty good time.

WHO GOES UP?

How's a dirtbag like me end up in a place like this? Been saved, man. I mean, I was my congregation's number one snake handler.

—ASH, "DARK SIDE OF THE MOON" (5-16)

Rules and concepts regarding the "what, why, and how" of who gets into Heaven are ever evolving. Ever since there has been a concept of the afterlife, there have been varying rules about how one got there. Among ancient cultures, there was often a different afterlife for different types of people. The Norse, for example, had a Heaven for warriors and/or those who died bravely—Valhalla. The Greeks had an underworld, the necropolis ruled by Hades, as well as a paradisiacal afterlife called Elysium.

Even when it comes to the Christian Heaven, there is no real consensus on what qualifies a person for entrance into the "pearly gates." Some denominations claim that a person must be baptized (a ceremony in which the adherent is ceremonially dipped into water as a symbol of spiritual purification and rebirth) in order to go to Heaven. Other denominations claim that one must only believe in Jesus in order to gain access to an eternity in Heaven.

Today, more and more people have begun to adopt a viewpoint that is sometimes called universalism or all paths to God. This view claims that all religions seek to understand God and that no single religious belief is any more or less valid than any other. In *Supernatural*, it would stand to reason that this is the point of view they used to create their rules about Heaven. This is made evident when Ash explains that he has visited the Heaven of Vatsyayana, the author of the Kama Sutra. Since Vatsyayana was of the Hindu Dharma faith, and is spending eternity in his own (as Ash puts it) "sweaty and confusing" Heaven, then it would stand to reason that adherence to any form of Judeo-Christianity would not be a prerequisite for getting into the place.

If one does get into Heaven, I guess death doesn't seem like all that big of a deal, especially judging from the following dialogue:

> DEAN: If it makes you feel any better, we got Ash killed, too.
> ASH: I'm *COOL* with it!
> DEAN: He's cool with it.
> —DEAN WINCHESTER AND ASH,
> "DARK SIDE OF THE MOON" (5-16)

Then again, it's probably a little hard to hold a grudge when you're living in a state of eternal bliss.

JOSHUA THE BRANCH AND HEAVEN'S GARDEN

> At the center of it all is the Magic Kingdom . . . the Garden.
> —ASH, "DARK SIDE OF THE MOON" (5-16)

In "Dark Side of the Moon," you may have noticed that Joshua is not like the other angels. Well, that's because he isn't like them (or, at least, he hasn't always been one of them). In the Old Testament Judeo-Christian book of the prophet Zechariah, there is mention of a "high priest" named Joshua being given a special place in Heaven. Joshua, unlike the other angels, was once a human being (if, of course, the character in *Supernatural* is the same Joshua mentioned in Zechariah).

Evidence of this can be found in the following excerpt of one particular vision of the prophet Zechariah:

> *And he showed me Joshua the high priest standing before the angel of the Lord, and Satan* [sometimes "the adversary" or "accusing angel"] *standing at his right side to accuse him. The Lord said to Satan, "The Lord rebukes you, Satan! The Lord who has chosen Jerusalem, rebukes you! Is not this man a burning stick snatched from the fire?"*
>
> *Now Joshua was clothed in filthy garments as he stood before the angel. The angel said to those standing before him, "Remove his filthy clothes." Then he said to Joshua, "See, I have taken away your iniquity, and will dress you in a change of clean and rich garments." Then I* [Zechariah] *said, "Put a clean turban* [sometimes "mitre" or "crown"] *on his head." So they put a clean turban on his head and clothed him, while the angel of the Lord stood by.*
>
> *The angel of the Lord gave this charge to Joshua: "This is what the Lord Almighty says: 'If you will walk in my ways and keep my charge, then you will govern my house and have charge of my courts, and I will give you a place among these standing here.'"*
>
> —ZECHARIAH 3:1–7

The identity of the Joshua mentioned in the above citation and the significance of his mention are both matters of some debate. Some claim that Joshua was a high priest who had perhaps been accused of rebelling (maybe by creating his own sect of the monotheistic YHVH/Jehovah cult of the Jews). However, this would not seem to make sense considering how he is exalted with a heavenly position in the text. Some claim that this may be because Joshua repented of his rebellion and returned to traditional Judaism. Others have claimed that "Joshua the high priest" was not supposed to be a literal person at all, but that this name and title were instead intended to serve as a metaphor for the entire nation of Israel. Arguing either of these points of view will result in no definitive proof.

If one considers the last few lines of the excerpt, however, Joshua's role as an angel in *Supernatural* begins to make sense. That Joshua will govern God's "house" and "have charge of [his] courts" would certainly seem to match up with the role of *Supernatural*'s Joshua. After all, Joshua explains to Sam and Dean that Heaven's "garden" is not necessarily a garden at all but is instead unique to each person:

> **You see what you want to here. For some, it's God's throne room, for others it's Eden. You two . . . I believe it's the Cleveland Botanical Gardens. You came here on a field trip.**
> —JOSHUA, "DARK SIDE OF THE MOON" (5-16)

Normally, it is understood that humans cannot become angels. Some say that this is because humans were granted souls, while angels were not. Maybe this is why, in *Supernatural*, it seems that the angel Zachariah looks down on Joshua. Perhaps this is because Joshua was not "born an angel," so to speak, but was once a human being. This would certainly make the man stand apart from the rest of the heavenly ranks.

While it is not normal for humans to become angels, the same cannot be said of the demons in the *Supernatural* mythos. In the universe of *Supernatural*, every soul that descends into the fiery pit of Hell will eventually become corrupted by it and, as Ruby once explained to Dean, will be transformed into "something else"— meaning demons. As we will see in the next chapter, these evil spirits revel in the corruption and torment of humans. However, as the Winchesters prove time and time again, some humans choose to fight back.

≡ 7 ≡

DEMONIC POSSESSIONS AND EXORCISMS

She's possessed. That's a human possessed by a demon, can't you tell?

—BOBBY SINGER, "DEVIL'S TRAP" (1-22)

D emonic possession has become an increasingly regular occurrence in *Supernatural*, with Sam and Dean frequently performing exorcisms of possessed individuals. The mythology of the show often plays with traditional notions of possession and exorcism in order to create an entirely new spin on an age-old idea. While the demons of *Supernatural* are a new creation, various rites for demonic exorcism have existed among many culture groups, from all over the globe, for thousands of years.

DEMONIC POSSESSION

Demonic possessions happen pretty fast on *Supernatural*. Some random guy can just be walking along, minding his own business, when a black cloud of demon shoves its way down his throat, and presto! He is possessed. His eyes turn black (or red or white, or whatever color fits the possessing demon), and now he has to suffer through watching every terrible thing the demon does while riding around in his body, powerless to do anything about it. Talk about a crappy deal.

In reality, recorded cases suggest that possession usually takes a little longer than what is portrayed on *Supernatural*. No fault of the show's, of course, because if we had to sit through the lengthy escalation of possession every time a demon tried to take a ride in someone's meat suit the show would get boring pretty quick.

Most demonologists would agree that possessions occur in progressive stages over a period of time. There are almost no recorded cases of an immediate possession, at least not for those who are possessed involuntarily.

This is one of the places where *Supernatural* deviates a bit from the lore. On the show, a demon can force its way into a person while an angel has to be given permission. In reality, the "rules" usually state the exact opposite. Angels, for the most part, don't need to occupy bodies because they are commonly believed to be able to transubstantiate. That is, they can change from "spirit form" to "physical form." Demons, on the other hand, have to find a way to get in, and they usually do this by exploiting one or more of the target individual's vices, personal weaknesses, or desires. Even when the demon initially gets in, it does not exercise much control over the person.

Cases of demonic possession generally follow three progressive stages:

Stage 1: Demonization

Stage 2: Personal possession

Stage 3: Perfect possession

Demonization refers to a period of time when a demon is testing you out, trying to find some kind of moral or spiritual weakness to exploit that will allow it to gain access to you. Sometimes the demon will stick around for years this way. Other times, it will either be scared off by prayer, exorcism, or something else it doesn't like, or it will become bored and move on (though the first scenario is a lot more likely).

In the latter parts of this stage, the demon will begin to make its way into the person's body. Its control is erratic but identifiable, and the possessed person begins to undergo subtle but uncharacteristic changes in mood, behavior, and personality. For example, the person may become unreasonably irritable. He or she might start displaying an aversion to anything having to do with faith, religion, or spirituality, avoiding, for example, prayers, relics, churches, temples, and even the names of angels. Demons have been documented as experiencing extreme discomfort in the presence of just about anything having to do with a spiritual practice (that is nondemonic, of course). The nice thing (if you can call it that) about this stage of possession is that something as simple as a prayer, blessing, or some purification ceremony is usually enough to expel the demon. Once it gets to the next stage, though, things get a little more difficult.

Personal possession refers to a situation in which the demon has come to exploit some flaw, likely the one it used to gain access to the victim, and twisted it so that he or she becomes dependent on its availability (think about how Ruby got Sam hooked on demon blood—different situation but the same general philosophy). The demon is then able to start taking more control over the body and begins gaining more influence, though sporadic it may be, over the person's physical actions. At this point the possessed person's will has begun to be overtaken by the demon.

The longer the demon remains in the victim, the more extreme the situation gets. For example, one of the most common traits of people experiencing personal possession is the spontaneous ability to understand or speak languages that are unknown to them. Another is having inexplicable knowledge of events they did not witness and of which they could not possibly have previous knowledge. For example, the possessed person might know that an acquaintance has a meeting to attend without being told. Of course, this knowledge could also be the result of premonitions, so it shouldn't be your sole criteria for claiming someone is possessed. Expelling a demon at this stage is still fairly routine. The victim may require an exorcism, but it will be easier to perform now than in the next stage. This is because the possessed person still has the majority of control over his or her will and can therefore participate in the exorcism. Once a possessed person reaches the third and final stage of perfect possession, things start to go seriously downhill—fast.

By the time a person reaches the stage of perfect possession, he or she is in some serious trouble. This stage, one should note, is the most similar to what one sees on *Supernatural*. Little if any of the possessed person's own will remains. More or less, the demon is calling the shots at this point.

The really creepy part is that people who experience perfect possession often militantly resist exorcism and usually behave as though they have accepted the demon within them. This is due to the fact that the person has developed a spiritual attachment to, and mental and emotional dependence on, the demon. This causes the person to experience feelings of extreme anxiety when it comes to expelling the demon. The demon has actually convinced the possessed person that he or she *needs* it in order to live a happy life.

Needless to say, cases of perfect possession are generally thought of as the most dangerous. The real danger comes from the fact that the demon doesn't mind hurting the exorcist or the possessed individual on its way out. For any legitimate exorcist, engaging a demon who has achieved perfect possession is a tricky situation that requires detailed planning. This is because once an exorcism begins it cannot be stopped until the demon is out. If, as sometimes happens, the exorcist is injured or breaks down and cannot continue, then a new exorcist must be on hand to finish the job. Perfect possession exorcisms are undertaken with extreme caution, because if mistakes are made in these extreme cases, they can actually prove to be fatal—for both the exorcist as well as the possessed individual.

Another point of contrast between *Supernatural* and real demonic possessions has to do with exorcisms. In the show, the simple recitation of an exorcism rite is usually enough to cast out a demon. Also, there are rarely if ever any repercussions for the one performing the recitation. Real exorcists, however, enter into direct confrontations with the spiritual agents of ultimate evil. Exorcism is an endeavor filled with dangers and pitfalls, and only those with the proper training and experience should ever attempt to perform one. Once an exorcism has begun, for example, the exorcist is in it until it's over.

In some cases, even successful exorcisms have left the acting exorcists with permanent psychological, and even physical, scars. A failed exorcism can be even worse. Failure can mean death, for both the exorcist and the possessed individual. Needless to say, being an exorcist is not an occupation one should enter into lightly.

PROTECTION AGAINST THE DEMONIC

There's no demon in her. There's no demon getting in her.
—DEAN WINCHESTER, "PHANTOM TRAVELER" (1-4)

The best defense is a good offense, right? Well, the good news is that there are tons of ways to protect yourself from demonic influence. Just about any object of faith—crosses, amulets, pictures of saints, and so on—can be used. This includes similar objects from any religion (as long as it is your religion, of course). Prayers also tend to make demons uncomfortable and encourage them to set up shop elsewhere.

When the demon doesn't take the hint, however, you might

need to pull out the big guns. One of the most common commands used to ward off demons has actually been used at least once on *Supernatural* and comes from a myth about the monk Saint Benedict.

THE SAINT BENEDICT EXORCISM

SAM: What if she's already possessed?
DEAN: There's ways to test that. I brought holy water.
SAM: No. I think we can go more subtle. If she's possessed, she'll flinch at the name of God.
—SAM AND DEAN WINCHESTER, "PHANTOM TRAVELER" (1-4)

Saint Benedict is viewed as one of the most powerful Roman Catholic saints when it comes to dealing with demonic powers. This is because he is said to have had a certain knack for bashing the devil over the head with his own tricks. A manuscript discovered in 1417 tells the story of a particular situation in which an agent of evil attempted to murder the monk by offering him poison. Because of the crude nature of medical science, and the fact that criminal forensics was not yet even invented, poisoning was a favored technique of assassins of the period.

According to the story, Benedict had been invited under false pretenses to the table of a man who was in fact an agent of the devil. The man first offered the monk a goblet of poisoned wine. Benedict made the sign of the cross, at which point the goblet immediately shattered as if it had been smashed with a hammer, even though nothing had touched it. Next the man offered a loaf of poisoned bread to the monk. As Benedict reached for it, a raven descended and flew off with it. In this manner, the assassination attempt was thwarted.

Benedict wasn't done with this guy, however—not by a long shot. Realizing that God had twice intervened to prevent him from consuming what he'd been offered, Benedict saw the situation for what it was. He stood and, with the following words, rebuked the demonic forces that controlled the man:

> *Vade retro Satana!*
> *Numquam suade mihi vana.*
> *Sunt mala quae libas.*
> *Ipse venena bibas!*

> *Step back, Satan/adversary!*
> *Tempt me not with vain things.*
> *What you offer is evil.*
> *Drink the poison yourself!*

Knowing they were beaten, the demonic forces made a hasty exit.

Even today, objects called Saint Benedict Medals are commonly used for protection against evil and demonic spirits. These roughly coin-sized medals depict the end scene of the previously mentioned story on one side, and on the other side are the letters VRS-NSMV-SMQL-IVB. These letters were first discovered written on the wall of Benedict's monastery, but no one knew what they meant until the previously mentioned manuscript was discovered.

SUPERNATURAL AND THE RITUALE ROMANUM RITES OF EXORCISM

MEG: An exorcism? Are you serious?

DEAN: Oh, we're going for it, baby. Head spinning . . . projectile vomiting . . . the whole nine yards.

—DEAN WINCHESTER AND MEG, "DEVIL'S TRAP" (1-22)

The Latin exorcisms used in *Supernatural* appear to be combinations of various exorcist rites used in Christianity over the years. The bulk of them come from the *Rituale Romanum* (Roman Ritual), a text of the Roman Catholic Church meant to serve as a sort of guidebook to priests. You won't find it in the new versions of the text, however, as the rite was seriously revised back in 1998. While it is nearly impossible to tell you exactly what version or exorcism rite is being used (it changes constantly on the show), we can at least offer you a copy of the common Latin recitations used in the original Roman Rite of Exorcism. Please note that this is just the recitation, not the rite in its entirety. Since full translations of the rite are rather rare, this might be a good time for you to start brushing up on your Latin. However, the text also warns that only appropriately trained exorcists, who have been given proper approval, should attempt to use this.

Deus, et pater Domini nostri Jesu Christi, invoco nomen sanctum tuum, et clementiam tuam supplex exposco: ut adversus hunc, et omnem immundum spiritum, qui vexat hoc plasma

*tuum. mihi auxilium praestare igneris. Per eumdem Dominum.
Amen.*

*Exorcizo te, immundissime spiritus, omnis incursio adversa-
rii, omne phantasma, omnis legio, in nomine Domini nostri Jesu
Christi eradicare, et effugare ab hoc plasmate Dei. Ipse tibi imperat, qui te de supernis caelorum in inferiora terrae demergi
praecepit. Ipse tibi imperat, qui mari, ventis, et tempestatibus
impersvit. Audi ergo, et time, satana, inimice fidei, hostis generis humani, mortis adductor, vitae raptor, justitiae declinator,
malorum radix, fomes vitiorum, seductor hominum, proditor
gentium, incitator invidiae, origo avaritiae, causa discordiae,
excitator dolorum: quid stas, et resistis, cum scias. Christum Dominum vias tuas perdere? Illum metue, qui in Isaac immolatus
est, in joseph venumdatus, in sgno occisus, in homine crucifixus,
deinde inferni triumphator fuit. Sequentes cruces fiant in fronte
obsessi. Recede ergo in nomine Patris et Filii, et Spiritus Sancti:
da locum Spiritui Sancto, per hoc signum sanctae Cruci Jesu
Christi Domini nostri: Qui cum Patre et eodem Spiritu Sancto
vivit et regnat Deus, Per omnia saecula saeculorum. Amen.*

*Domine, exaudi orationem meam. Et clamor meus ad te
veniat. Dominus vobiscum. Et cum spiritu tuo.*

*Deus, conditor et defensor generis humani, qui hominem ad
imaginem tuam formasti; respice super hunc famulum tuum,
qui dolis immundi spiritus appetitur, quem vetus adversarius,
antiquus hostis terrae, formidinis horrore circumvolat, et sen-
sum mentis humanae stupore defigit, terrore contrubat, et metu
trepidi timoris exagitat. Repelle, Domine, virtutem diaboli, fal-
lacesque ejus insidias amove:*

Procul impius tentator aufugiat: sit nominis tui signo famu-

lus tuus munitus et in animo tutus et corpore. Tu pectoris hujus interna custodias. Tu viscera regas. Tu cor confirmes. In anima adversarius potestatis tentamenta evanescant. Da, Domine, ad hanc invocationem sanctissimi nominis tui gratiam, ut, qui hucusque terrebat, territus aufugiat, et victus abscedat, tibique possit hic famulus tuus et corde firmatus et mente sincerus, debitum praebere famulatum. Per Dominum. Amen.

Adjuro te, serpens antique, per judicem vivorum et mortuorum, per factorem tuum, per factorem mundi, per eum, qui habet potestatem mittendi te in gehennam, ut ab hoc famulo Dei, ad Ecclesiae sinum recurrit, cum metu, et exercitu furoris tui festinus discedas. Adjuro te iterum non mea infirmitate, sed virtute Spiritus Sancti, ut exeas ab hoc famulo Dei, quem omnipotens Deus ad imaginem suam fecit. Cede igitur, cede non mihi, sed ministro Christi. Illius enim te urget potestas, qui te Cruci suae subjugavit. Illius brachium contremisce, qui devictis gemitibus inferni, animas ad lucem perduxit. Sit tibi terror corpus hominis, sit tibi formido imago Dei. Non resistas, nec moreris discedere ab homine isto, quoniam complacuit Christo in homine habitare. Et ne contemnendum putes, dum me peccatorem nimis esse cognoscis. Imperat tibi Deus. Imperat tibi majestas Christi Imperat tibi Deus Pater, imoerat tibi Deus Filius, imperat tibi Deus Spiritus Sanctus. Imperat tibi sacramentum Crucis. Imperat tibi fides sanctorum Apostolorum Petri et Pauli, et ceterorum Sanctorum. Imperat tibi Martyrum sanguis, Imperat tibi contentia Confessorum. Imperat tibi pia Sanctorum et Sanctarum omnium intercessio, Imperat tibi christianae fidei mysteriorum virtus. Exi ergo, transgressor. Exi, seducor, plene omni dolo et fallacia, virtutis inimice, innocentium perse-

cutor. Da locum, dirissime, da loocum, impiissime, da locum Christo, in quo nihil invevisti de operibus tuis: qui te spoliavit, qui regnum tuum destruxit, qui te victum ligavit, et vasa tua diripuit: qui te projecit in tenebras exteriores, ubi tibi cum ministris tuis erit praeparatus interitus. Sed quid truculente reniteris? Quid temerarie detrectas? Reus es omnipotenti Deo, cujus statuta transgressus es. Reus es Filio ejus Jesu Christo Domino nostro, quem tentare ausus es, et crucifigere praesumpsisti. Reus es humano generi, cui tuis persua- sionibus mortis venenum propinasti. Adjuro ergo te, draco nequissime, in nomine Agni immaculati, qui ambulavit super aspidem et basiliscum, qui conculavit leonem et draconem, ut discedas ab hoc homine, discedas ab Ecclesia Dei: contremisce, et effuge, invocato nomine Domini illius, quem inferi tremunt: cui Virtutes caelorum, et Potestates, et Dominationes subjectae sunt: quem Cherubim et Serpahim indefessis vocibus laudant, dicentes: Sanctus, sanctus, sanctus Dominus Deus Sabaoth. Imperat tibi Verbum caro factum. Imperat tibi natus ex Virgine. Imperat tibi Jesus Nazarenus, qui te, cum disciplulos ejus contemneres, elisum atque prostratum exire praecepit ab homine: quo praesente, cum te ab homine serparasset, nec porcorum gregem ingredi praesumebas. Recede ergo nunc adjuratus in nomine ejus ab homine, quem ipse plasmavit. Durum est tibi velle resistere. Durum est tibi contra stimulum calcitrare, Quia quanto tardius exis, tanto magis tibi supplicium crescit, quia non homines contemnis, sed illum, qui dominatur vivorum et mortuorum, qui venturus est judicare vivos et mortuos, et saeculum per ignem. Amen.

*Domine, exaudi orationem meam. Et clamor meus ad te
veniat. Dominus vobiscum Et cum spiritu tuo.*

*Deus caeli, Deus terrae, Deus Angelorum, Deus Archange-
lorum, Deus Prophetarum, Deus Apostolorum, Deus Martyrum, Deus Virginum, Deus, qui potestatem habes donare
vitam post mortem, requiem post laborem: quia non est alius
Deus praeter te, nec esse poterit verus, nisi tu, Creator caeli et
terrae, qui verus Rex es, et cujus regni non erit finis; humiliter
majestati gloriae tuae supplico, ut hunc famulum tuum de im-
mundis spiritibus liberare digneris. Per Christum Dominum
Nostrum. Amen.*

Here is a translation of the first few paragraphs, since translat-
ing the entire thing would be incredibly lengthy:

*I exorcise you, unclean spirit. Every incursion of the opposite
party is every specter from Hell, every legion, rooted up in the
name of our Lord Jesus Christ, driven away from this creature
of God. He commands you, who was with you and cast you
from Heaven into the lower parts of the Earth. He commands
you, creature of the sea, to the winds, and a storm impervious.
Hearken, therefore, and tremble in fear, Satan, enemy of the
faith, the enemy of the human race, of the death being drawn
back, a robber of life, of justice, you root of all evil and vice,
seducer of men, the traitor of the nations, instigator of envy, the
origin of their greed, the cause of discord, and maker of sorrows:
Why are you standing, and resist, knowing as you must that
Christ the Lord will destroy thy ways? The one you fear, who in*

Isaac was sacrificed, in Joseph sold, was killed as a sign, in the body of a man was crucified, and gained victory over Hell. Get thee back, therefore, in the name of the Father, the son, and the Holy Ghost: give place to the Holy Spirit, by the words of Jesus on the cross, by the sign of the holy Christ, Our Lord who with the Father and in the same Holy Spirit lives and reigns, God forever, world without end. Amen.

O Lord, hear my prayer. And let my cry come unto thee. May the Lord be with you and amend your spirit.

And the defender God, creator of the human race, "that man is formed according to your image": look down upon this your servant, the unclean spirits within, who desire to deceive, whom the old adversary attacks, the old adversary of the Earth, surrounded by fear and horror, and astonishes the soul, and causes the mind to fear, and starts the body to trembling.

[Please note that the above interpretation is not the authorized translation commonly used by the church.]

DEMONS SUCK AT MATH

In *Supernatural*, demonic possession basically occurs in a sort of one-to-one fashion, meaning one demon to each human possessed. However, in many cases of possession it is not one demon but many who take up residence in a single human body. Physical concepts like numbers don't really apply to nonphysical beings such as demons.

This element of demonic possession is well illustrated by a

story from the New Testament of the Christian Bible, in which Jesus encounters a possessed man in Mark 5:1–9. The demons within the man recognize Jesus, and he rushes up begging for mercy. When Jesus demands a name from the demons possessing the man, he receives the reply, "My name is Legion, for we are many." Jesus then casts the demons out of the man and into a herd of pigs, which then run into the sea and drown themselves. And what did Jesus get for his troubles? He got asked to leave town. Apparently, even the Messiah had trouble with the locals sometimes. Hunters can relate to that, right?

When it comes to dealing with demons, there are a good many that hunters probably would rather not come up against—Azazel and Alastair, for example. But there is one scary bitch who easily puts both of them to shame. Her name is Lilith, and you don't want to get on her bad side.

≋ 8 ≋

LILITH IS ONE SCARY BITCH

Look. Lilith is one scary bitch. When I was in the pit, there was talk. She's cooking up something big—apocalyptic big.
—RUBY, "I KNOW WHAT YOU DID LAST SUMMER" (4-9)

R uby wasn't kidding when she said Lilith was "one scary bitch." After all, what's creepier than a demonic chick who possesses innocent young girls, slaughters people by the dozens, eats babies, and whose idea of vacation is possessing the young daughter of a suburbanite family and then tormenting them for days while she kills them off one by one. Lilith . . . yeah, she is not a nice lady.

The demonic character Lilith, as she is portrayed in *Supernatural*, has her origins in the very earliest days of human myth and civilization. In fact, it is now speculated by many mythology and history scholars that Lilith was once a major deity in the pantheon of a now-lost prehistoric civilization. The oldest evidence of Lilith that has survived the passage of time is a four-thousand-year-old series of clay tablets, commonly called the Tablets of Inanna.

Lilith's portrayal in *Supernatural* is primarily based on her later depictions in Judaic mythology. However, even in Judaism it is said that Lilith was once human (which is in line with the show's mythos that demons were originally human). In fact, according to a number of apocryphal or, at best, noncanonical Judaic texts, Lilith was the first wife of Adam and therefore the first woman to be created.

ANCIENT SUMERIAN, AKKADIAN, AND BABYLONIAN LILITH DEPICTIONS

And it is written, that the first demon will be the last seal. And you busted her open.

—RUBY, "LUCIFER RISING" (4-22)

While the Lilith character of *Supernatural* is heavily based on her portrayals in Judaic demonology as a seductress with a penchant for infanticide, she is actually older than even Judaism. In fact, the first myth to mention Lilith's name is found in the Tablets of Inanna, some of the oldest existing written works in human history. Many of the stories from these tablets tell of the exploits of an ancient Mesopotamian goddess named Inanna. The tablets that survive today are dated at roughly between 2000 BCE and 1950 BCE. These clay tablets have been a matter of close study and debate ever since the first of them were found during the initial excavations of ancient Mesopotamian cities such as Ur and Uruk in the mid-nineteenth century, smack dab in the middle of modern-day Iraq, Iran, and Syria.

Believe it or not, the surviving tablets are not likely to be the oldest written accounts of these ancient stories; they are just the oldest that have survived. Scholars now believe that these tablets were copied and/or updated from an original set that was probably transcribed by Sumerian scribes sometime around 4000 BCE, and those were likely recorded from an even older orally conveyed version of the story. Most known myths originate from oral traditions long before being first written down. These ancient tablets were composed with a system of writing known as cuneiform, whereby characters were composed in wedge-shaped forms. Cuneiform, a written pictographic language (in which symbols represent words instead of sounds), was originally developed by the ancient Sumerians but was later forcefully adapted into a phonetic alphabet by the Akkadians for use with their own language, Akkad or *Agade*. This system of writing consists of tiny wedges and lines that can be combined in a variety of ways in order to make symbols. A small, flat stick, or stylus, was used to make indentations into slabs of wet clay that then hardened into solid tablets, which could be cataloged and preserved.

One myth from these tablets, sometimes called "Inanna and the *Huluppu* Tree" or "The *Huluppu* Story/Myth," is part of a larger ancient Mesopotamian creation myth. In fact, it may have been one of the first primal myths to be written down. Because of a number of striking similarities, many scholars now believe that the Judeo-Christian Eden story was likely inspired by or modeled after a number of elements from the *huluppu* tree story.

The story tells of how there was once a special tree, called the *huluppu*, which grew along the fertile banks of the Euphrates River. However, one day the South Wind blew in and uprooted the tree, sending it floating along the waters of the Euphrates. Eventually, a young goddess finds the tree as she walks alongside the river (she is unnamed in the myth, but it is generally believed that this figure is likely Geshtinanna, who served as handmaiden to the goddess Inanna). The goddess pulls the tree from the waters and is urged by the gods Anu (god of the sky/heavens) and Enlil (god of air/wind/breath) to take the *huluppu* tree to the great garden of Inanna located in the city of Uruk. Inanna receives the tree from the goddess and has it replanted in her splendid garden. Inanna tends the tree with a little tender loving care and decides that she will give it another ten years so that it can grow to maturity. Inanna's intention is to use the wood of the *huluppu* to construct for herself a throne and bed.

When the ten years are up, Inanna returns to the *huluppu* tree. However, she is horrified to discover that she is prevented from approaching it owing to the fact that three rather nasty figures have taken up residence in it. Over the years, you see, a "snake/serpent that could not be charmed" had built a nest at the tree's roots. In the branches of the tree, Inanna found that a powerful creature known as the Anzu (or Zu bird, which was a mythical winged creature that was often portrayed somewhat like a winged lion, other times as a kind of cross between a sphinx and a gryphon) was raising its young there. To make matters worse, the "dark maiden" known as Lilith had made a home of the *huluppu's* trunk. Inanna wept, realizing that she did not have the power (though the reasons for her powerlessness are unspecified) to remove these unwanted guests from her beloved *huluppu* tree.

Luckily, Inanna's brother Gilgamesh hears of his poor sister's situation and comes to help her out. He takes up his heavy shield and ax and rushes in with a warrior's fury. With his giant bronze ax that weighs "7 talents and 7 minas" (in modern terms, this adds up to just over *475 pounds!*), Gilgamesh slays the serpent that couldn't be charmed. Seeing this, the Anzu bird flies away with its young. Lilith, terrified by Gilgamesh's fury, tears down her own home. She then flees from the *huluppu* and goes away to the "wild uninhabited lands."

Now that the *huluppu* has been cleansed of all unwelcomed inhabitants, Gilgamesh loosens the tree's roots and, with help from the "sons of the city" (meaning the young men/warriors of Uruk), cuts the mighty branches from the trunk. The *huluppu* is then used to make a throne and bed for Inanna, as she'd planned, as well as a number of additional luxuries, tools, and similar useful items considered to be symbols of ancient Sumerian civilization.

The above story obviously bears a number of elements that are comparable to those of the Judeo-Christian story of Eden from Genesis:

1. A special tree

2. A "garden," in which the special tree is planted

3. Presence of a snake or serpent

4. Forced exile from the garden by a patriarchal god

5. Conflict between man/god, woman/goddess, and an evil entity

THE EXPULSION OF LILITH

The expulsion of Lilith from the *huluppu* tree (and, by association, the cities of ancient Mesopotamia) marks the beginning of a theme that has stayed with her throughout the available Lilith mythology. Across the board, Lilith is portrayed as a troublesome goddess or woman, a dark maiden who must be expelled by a patriarchal deity or male sky god. While next to nothing is known about Lilith's true origins, this reoccurring theme actually serves as a clue that suggests she may have once been very important to one or more ancient, possibly prehistoric, culture groups.

In the ancient world, politics and religion were often one and the same thing. In an age of "god-kings," when rulers commonly deified themselves and were worshipped by their subjects, the creation of corresponding religious myths was often commissioned in order to validate the "godhoods" of those who founded or ruled over ancient cities.

While the formation of cities stands as a landmark in the advancement of human civilization, these walled settlements were sources of conflict as well as frequent targets for raids and violent campaigns of conquest. And for thousands of years, the cities of ancient Mesopotamia passed from one ruling culture group to another. The Al-Ubaid people, believed to have been among the first to conquer agriculture (but, apparently, not warfare), were conquered and absorbed by the Sumerians, who were in turn conquered by the Akkadians, who were eventually forced out of power due to constant and frequent raids by nomadic Semitic tribes. The Sumerians took back the land for a brief period, until it was once again taken from them by an alliance of warring Assyrian-Semitic kings. These kings were eventually weakened by infighting (and, likely, inbreeding) and bouts of widespread civil unrest, which led to a period of violent warfare. When the smoke cleared, all that remained was the Babylonian Empire.

Since nearly all of these ancient Mesopotamian kings claimed to be gods or, at the least, the descendents of gods, conquered populations were left with a unique problem. Their thoughts might be explained as going something like this: "If our old god-king (may he rest in peace) was supposed to be all-powerful, then what does that make this new god-king?" The solution to this came in the form of myths that one might best categorize as "My deity beat up your deity." Many such myths exist, which tell of how the gods of a conquering culture group defeated and/or exiled the gods of the recently conquered culture. Even Christianity has given birth to myths of this nature. Saint Patrick, for example, is said to have exiled all of the snakes from the island of Ireland when he brought Christianity to the "pagan" Celts. Same song, new tune.

Considering all of this, Lilith's expulsion during the *huluppu* tree story gains a greater significance. Anzu and the snake/serpent that could not be charmed were mythical beasts likely associated with Lilith's cult (the word *cult*, when used to refer to ancient religions, does not have the negative modern connotations—it just means a religious group) before the Inanna stories were written.

Even in her Judaic form, Lilith is still associated with similar animals such as snakes and birds of prey. So why would the ancient scribes make a point of writing a story in which Lilith is exiled along with these mythical creatures? The answer is that she was likely the ruling deity of a popular cult from some preexisting culture group. And just as Lilith was defeated by a new pantheon of gods and goddesses, so were her followers defeated by a conquering society.

This exile element of the first-known Lilith myth could have been intended to send a very strong message to Lilith's followers: "Your goddess is no longer in the city. If you want to worship her, then you will need to leave." In the ancient world, cities offered safety, laws, and protection. Life outside was dangerous even for armed trade caravans, and traveling on one's own would have been nothing short of suicidal. During the period of the Sumer-Akkad Empire, it is likely that one ruler commissioned the writing of the *huluppu* tree myth in order to either forcefully convert or exile the remaining members of Lilith's popular goddess cult. However, we will discuss what may have happened to the exiled followers of Lilith later on in the chapter. For now, there is one more element to this myth that needs to be addressed.

Challengers to the idea of Lilith's prehistoric godhood often point to the fact that she is never directly referred to as a goddess in the *huluppu* tree myth. But while Lilith might not have been named as a goddess, the same cannot be said for Inanna, who is well known to have been a popular and powerful goddess in the pantheon of the Sumer-Akkad culture group. And yet Inanna does not have the power to banish Lilith from the tree on her own. This raises yet another very interesting question: why would a powerful goddess such as Inanna be unable to do something as simple as kick a dark maiden and a couple of her creepy pets out of a tree? The answer is quite simple: Lilith must be a goddess as well and therefore equal to or greater in strength than Inanna. So, in keeping with the patriarchal mind-set of the ruling Sumer-Akkad culture, only a male warrior god (in this case, Gilgamesh) would be powerful enough to do such a thing.

This brings us back to the question of how Lilith's cult survived her expulsion from the cradle of civilization. Let's examine what may have become of her loyal, exiled adherents. There are extensions of Lilith throughout world mythology . . . you just have to know how to look for her.

OTHER FACES OF LILITH

LILITH: Hi. I'm looking for two boys. One's really tall, and one's really cute.
NANCY: Well, what's your name sweetie?
LILITH: Lilith.

—LILITH AND NANCY, "JUS IN BELLO" (3-12)

So, just how did Lilith's name survive for so many years, when the names of the very gods who mythically banished her in the ancient Mesopotamian story were lost and rediscovered in only the last few centuries? Just as Lilith is able to change her appearance on *Supernatural*, the goddess Lilith managed to disguise herself in the mythological traditions of other culture groups. Obviously, Lilith eventually made her way into early Judaic mythology, but how?

One theory asserts that the remaining loyal followers of the Lilith cult chose to flee the cities of the Fertile Crescent. Some members went east until they eventually reached what is now India. Others likely traveled north along the Euphrates River until they reached the Taurus Mountains and were forced to turn west. They stopped once they reached the Mediterranean coastal region of Sidon and eventually came into contact with the seafaring Phoenicians. At this point, some Lilith cult followers may have chosen to stay and integrated themselves into the Phoenician group while others, it would seem, chose to continue traveling south along the Mediterranean coast. Unfortunately for these goddess worshippers, this journey brought them into the lands of Judea.

Judea may have actually been a brief safe haven for Lilith's expelled followers. However, it would soon become a very dangerous place for any religious group aside from the YHVH cult (now known as Judaism). During the time of the young King Josiah's reign, between 641 BCE and 609 BCE, the ruler of Judea began to strictly enforce the religion of the monotheistic YHVH cult. As part of this "religious reform," Josiah went on a bloody campaign of persecution in which he had the temples of all non-YHVH cults razed to the ground, their idols smashed, altars burned, and priests and priestesses executed. Needless to say, any remaining members of the Lilith cult would have suddenly found themselves in a terribly frightening and dangerous situation. As can be rather easily deduced from noncanonical Judaic writings about Lilith, she was mythically declared an enemy of YHVH and by association all of Judea. This likely encouraged the demonized form of the Lilith of Eden, which will be discussed in the next section of this chapter.

What of the other followers of the Lilith cult, however? What became of them? No one knows for sure, but there are linguistic clues that suggest Lilith may have been reborn elsewhere, transformed by the culture groups who came into contact with her loyalist exiles. This is where things get really interesting.

Lilith is known to have been referred to by three names in the dialects of the Sumer-Akkad region—Lilit (Sumerian), Lam (Akkad), and Kal (used in various East Mesopotamian dialects, mainly by those who resided on or near the eastern side of the Tigris River). These names are striking in their phonetic similarities to similar female mythical/religious figures among cultures that very well could have come into contact with the exiled followers of Lilith.

You will read more details about Kali, the Hindu Dharma goddess of death, destruction, and pestilence, in chapter 9, but it is possible that this frightening goddess is one of Lilith's later, non-Mesopotamian extensions.

The idea that trade and sharing occurred between ancient Mesopotamia and the Hindu Kush was long thought impossible by modern scholars. However, all of that changed when an ancient cylinder seal portraying a row of tusked elephants was discovered among ancient Sumerian ruins. There was just one issue with this: elephants are not indigenous to ancient Mesopotamia. So the only way someone would know what an elephant looked like would be if either he or she traveled to the neighboring Hindi region and saw one or a Hindi caravan brought elephants to the area.

The discovery of this seal stands as evidence that ancient trade routes were longer and far more developed than previously thought. This means that some form of passable route, likely used primarily by armed trading caravans, was in operation between the two countries. This also means that members of the exiled Lilith cult would have known of the route and perhaps chose to make new lives for themselves among the ancient Hindi culture groups, bringing with them their name for Lilith, a dark maiden who in their dialect was called Kal. As one will see in chapter 9 on ancient apocalyptic lore, Kali's skin is said to be the color of night or darkness. In fact, Kali is called the Dark/Black One.

Shortly before the time of its exile, the Lilith cult seems to have become integrated with that of a similar goddess named Lamashtu, who brought death and illness and had a thing for eating babies. This baby-killing element was likely modified by Hindi/Vedic myths, which claim that Kali was the first victim of infanticide.

Lilith's other name, Lam, may have further encouraged the confusion and integration between the Lilith and Lamashtu cults. Lam, likely from an Akkad dialect, may have been used by those of Lilith's followers who traveled west to the Mediterranean coastal areas of Sidon and Judea. As mentioned earlier, a portion of these exiles were likely absorbed by the seafaring Phoenician culture group, taking to the waters of the Mediterranean and further spreading their influence to the Minoans of Crete and other ancient Greek peoples.

Among the ruins of the Minoans, statues that depict a bare-breasted goddess/maiden holding snakes in both her hands have been excavated. Her posture bears similarities to reliefs and cylinder seal depictions that are believed to be of Lilith or Lamashtu. However, it is a Greek mythical figure who is of most interesting note—Lamia.

Greek myth describes Lamia as having once been human. Depending on which version you are reading, she was once a queen of Libya, Egypt, or Persia (to the Greeks, Mesopotamia came to be known as Persia). For reasons that differ from one version of the myth to the next, she was cursed by being transformed into a monstrous creature. Some versions say she had an illegitimate child with Zeus, whose wrathful wife, Hera, cursed her with a lust for the flesh of babies and thus caused her to eat her own child. While there may be differing reasons for her curse, most of the elements about what she became are fairly consistent. Homicidally insane, Lamia drank the blood of men she seduced, stole unattended babies from their cribs and ate them (again with the baby eating!), and was generally unpleasant in just about every way imaginable. Sounds a lot like the Lilith in *Supernatural*, doesn't she?

Speaking of Lilith, she is still around (in mythological terms, at least). Sometimes revered, sometimes demonized, Lilith has stood the test of time unlike any other known mythical figure. With six thousand to eight thousand years of mythological tradition under her belt, it is unlikely that any mythical figure will ever be found who can match her in this regard, which seems rather ironic considering the lengths to which so many culture groups have gone throughout the centuries in their attempts to get rid of her. For the most part, we have the mystical and noncanonical traditions of Judaism to thank for Lilith's preservation.

LILITH OF EDEN

Most people would probably say they know the Creation story. However, the standard version of this Judeo-Christian primal myth is likely an alteration of an older story that had some key differences. Why change it? Better yet, what was changed? The canonical version of the Eden story was likely changed for one very specific reason—to get rid of Lilith. Putting together how this happened requires a little detective work, however (you didn't think this was going to be easy, did you?).

Clues about Lilith's role in the original Eden story can even be found in the Judeo-Christian version of the myth. In Genesis, for example, on the sixth day of God's work, when the creation of humans is first mentioned, it is written, "Man and Woman, He created them." This is sort of odd when you consider that Eve (commonly thought of as the "first woman") doesn't actually show up until later on in the myth, when God does the whole "rib trick" thing. So this raises a question—who was this woman in the initial "Man and Woman" verse, if not Eve? Long story short . . . it was Lilith.

Many believe that evidence of Lilith's presence was removed from the Judaic canon around the time it was written down. However, the myth had long been conveyed by way of an oral tradition. After all, altering a myth may change what people read, but it cannot change what they already know. Despite her removal from the canonical texts, Lilith's name and stories survive in noncanonical texts such as the Zohar (or Book of Splendor), a text of the Judaic mystical practice of Kabala, and the Alpha Bet of Ben Sira.

The Alpha Bet of Ben Sira (also known as the Alpha Beta text) is a medieval manuscript written by a Jewish mystic named Ben Sira. While the text covers a variety of topics, it has received the most attention for one particular story—a retelling of the Genesis myth, one that includes a character absent from the canonical Judeo-Christian texts. Lilith.

No complete English translations of Ben Sira's Alpha Bet exist, though a number of academic texts reference translated excerpts, especially when it comes to the Lilith story.

The story goes that Ben Sira was serving as a mystic, adviser, and healer to a nobleman. When the nobleman's young son fell terribly ill, he demanded that Ben Sira heal the boy. The mystic drew a magical symbol on the floor beneath where the boy slept. When the nobleman inquired as to the symbol's meaning, most likely fearing that it was some dark magic, Ben Sira explained that it was a symbol to bar Lilith, a demon who brought illness and death to young children. The nobleman inquired further, demanding to know the origins of this Lilith demon, and so Ben Sira wrote down the story. While minor details change from one English language telling of the story to the next, the basic plotline remains the same.

The story, as told by Ben Sira, goes a little something like this:

Lilith is formed from the Earth in the same manner as Adam (hence the confusing "Man and Woman, He created them" verse in Genesis). Problems arise between the two inhabitants of Eden almost immediately. More or less, their feud comes to a head when Adam demands to be on top of Lilith, in the "dominant position" during sex. Lilith refuses to obey. Adam flies into a rage and tries to force himself on her, but she escapes his attempt at rape by calling out God's "Holy Name." By doing so, Lilith is rescued from the attack by the hand of God and ascends from Eden. Her escape is short lived, however, and God insists that she return to Eden and "play nice" with Adam. In the presence of the Almighty himself, Lilith again refuses to obey even

His orders. As punishment for rebelling against His demands, God casts Lilith from His divine presence and exiles her into the terrible wastelands that lie beyond the paradise of Eden. On top of this, He also curses Lilith with delivering one hundred still-born babies each day. She wanders from Eden into the direction of what will later be known as the Sea of Reeds.

In order that Lilith will be at least given a chance to repent of her rebellion (one has to admit, however, that agreeing to live with a guy who tried to rape you sounds less like rebellion and more like common sense), God sends three angels—Sanvi, Sansanvi, and Semangelaf—to offer her a chance to return to Eden, submit to the will of God, and be subservient to Adam. To put it simply, Lilith tells all three angels to shove it where the sun don't shine. The exchange between Lilith and these three angels reveals a number of things about her. Most translations are in line with the following excerpt:

God immediately sent three angels and told them: "Go and fetch Lilith; if she agrees to come, bring her, and if she does not, bring her by force." The three angels went . . . and caught up with her at the Sea [the Red Sea, or Sea of Reeds], in the place where the Egyptians were destined to die. They seized her and said to her: "If you will agree to come, then come. If not, we shall drown you in the sea." Lilith answered, "Darlings, I know myself that God created me only to afflict babies with fatal disease when they are eight days old; I shall have permission to harm them from their births until their eighth day of life and no longer when the baby is male; but when a baby is female, I shall have permission to afflict them for twelve days." The angels, however, would not leave her alone, not until she swore by the name of God that wherever she saw their names or likenesses in a writing or amulet, she would not possess or afflict the baby. She swore, and they then left her immediately.

This story is important because in a way it ties Lilith to her original *huluppu* tree myth. Ben Sira's Lilith of Eden, much like her *huluppu* tree predecessor, flies away from the violent attack of a male figure. In Ben Sira's tale, however, she is fleeing from Adam's attempt at forced sexual dominance instead of Gilgamesh's insanely heavy ax. In fact, most English translations of this part of Ben Sira's story say that Lilith "flew into the air and fled" after speaking the "Holy Name." This is interesting because in the *huluppu* story it is also written that Lilith "flew away and fled" into the wild when Gilgamesh advances with his weapon. Many scholars agree that it is more than likely that Ben Sira's story is his own telling of an original version of the Genesis myth.

LILITH THE BABY EATER

RUBY: I closed in on a member of Lilith's entourage. You might call her a . . . personal chef.

SAM: Chef? Seriously? . . . What does she eat?

RUBY: (shakes her head and grimaces with subtle disgust) You don't wanna know.

—SAM WINCHESTER AND RUBY,
"WHEN THE LEVEE BREAKS" (4-21)

As you read in the previous section's excerpt from Ben Sira's Alpha Bet, Lilith was only allowed to escape the wrath of the angels by agreeing not to do harm in any place where she saw an amulet or writing that depicted them or bore their names. For untold centuries, pregnant mothers in Judaic culture often wore small amulets inscribed with the names of these three angels. As time went on, the names of Adam and Eve became a common addition to these amulets. Finally, on a majority of these round amulets can be found an inscription that reads BARRING LILITH. Before a woman was about to give birth, it was common for Jewish midwives to inscribe symbols similar to those found on such amulets upon the floor of the delivery room with charcoal or chalk.

Her later identification as a "baby eater" likely came from Lilith's integration with Lamashtu. Lamashtu, on top of being a female spirit of pestilence, was also said to be especially fond of devouring infants. When the cults of these two figures merged, Lilith acquired the reputation for eating babies that follows her to this very day.

After her encounter with the three angels, in the Judaic story, Lilith jumped into the Red Sea. There is some lore that says that Lilith, and certain members of her demonic brood called *lilin* or *lilum*, lie in wait underwater and snatch away children who linger too close. Their helpless victims are dragged to the watery depths and, more often than not, eaten alive.

LILITH THE DEMON QUEEN

Judaic demonology and folklore states that it was in the depths of the sea that Lilith became the wife of one of the Four Demon

Princes of Hell, Samael, in his form as the "Slant Serpent" Leviathan, to which Lilith became the female version counterpart. The coupling of these two figures (male/Samael and female/Lilith) came to be called Leviathan, the name by which this creature is now known. During the end times, as written in the Old Testament book of Isaiah 27:1, "In that day God, with his mighty sword, shall punish Leviathan the piercing serpent, even Leviathan that Slant Serpent; and He shall slay the dragon that is in the sea."

Lilith is also identified in lore as the consort of another high-ranking Demon King by the name of Ashmodai. Her relationships with Samael and Ashmodai eventually led to her being split into two forms in the lore—"Great Lilith/Grandmother Lilith" as the wife of Samael, and "Maiden Lilith" as the wife of Ashmodai. Interestingly enough, it is said that these two Liliths do not get along with one another. However, on the final Day of Atonement, they will return to their original wholeness and become Lilith as the Demon Queen, of whom it is written, "Lilith and her four hundred and twenty demonic legions shall march out from the deserts." And Lilith the Demon Queen, it is said, will be right out front . . . her voice shattering the air as she screeches in delight.

However, Lilith is not the only ancient mythological figure who has a bone to pick when it comes to the Judeo-Christian Apocalypse. As you will see in the next chapter, just about every major culture group on Earth has its own take on how the human world finally gets obliterated. And, as one might expect, it rarely ends pretty.

≈ 9 ≈

ANCIENT ORIGINS OF A FUTURE APOCALYPSE

I mean, screw the angels and the demons and their crap Apocalypse. They want to fight a war, they can find their own planet. This one's ours, and I say they get the hell off it. We take 'em all on. We kill the devil. Hell, we even kill Michael if we have to. But we do it our damn selves.

—DEAN WINCHESTER, "SYMPATHY FOR THE DEVIL" (5-1)

Sam and Dean spend a good amount of their time and energy trying to prevent the world from coming to a bloody and violent end. However, myth tells us that the Winchester gang may just be fighting a losing battle. The idea of the Apocalypse is nothing new, after all. In fact, a large majority of the human race has been looking forward to a future doom for thousands of years. Perhaps, in the end, there is no way to permanently stop the world from ending. Maybe the Apocalypse can only be postponed.

Spookily enough, the apocalyptic myths of most world religions agree that in the end, just as the mythos of *Supernatural* portrays, the celestial forces of good and evil will eventually clash in a final battle that will bring an end to the world as we know it. The Apocalypse is not an exclusively Judeo-Christian affair, however, and the writers of *Supernatural* address this issue in season 5, episode 19, "Hammer of the Gods," in which many figures from pre-Christian religions assemble in order to halt the Christian Armageddon jump-started by a group of powerful but rogue archangels.

THE BATTLE BETWEEN GOOD AND EVIL: AHURA MAZDA VERSUS ANGRA MAINYU

It's uh . . . turns out it's Zoroastrian. Very, very old school . . . like two thousand years before Christ.

—SAM WINCHESTER, "SHADOW" (1-16)

Supernatural portrays the Christian Apocalypse as a final showdown between two of God's most powerful creations, the warrior archangel Michael and the rebellious fallen archangel Lucifer (for more information, see chapters 3 and 4). However, this concept of the world being destroyed during a final battle between good and evil forces is not a new one. In fact, it has its origins in what is thought to be one of the world's earliest monotheistic religions.

An ancient prophet by the name of Zoroaster (or, in the original Persian, Zarathustra) was likely among the first, if not *the* first, to dichotomize the divine forces as "good" and "evil." Zoroaster, who is generally believed to have lived sometime between 1700 BCE and 1200 BCE, portrayed these forces as a battle in which a benevolent god named Ahura Mazda wages a constant war against a malevolent god named Angra Mainyu. In the early beliefs of Zoroastrianism both Ahura Mazda and Angra Mainyu were seen as nearly equal creator gods. While Ahura Mazda created life, light, and all things good, his counterpart Angra Mainyu created demons, darkness, and all things evil.

While Zoroastrianism eventually came to resemble a more monotheistic belief system, in which the one god Ahura Mazda was worshipped, this was not the case in the earlier years of the religion's development. History tells us that prior to the arrival of the prophet Zoroaster the Indo-Iranian people worshipped Ahura Mazda in a polytheistic form, as one god among others.

Zoroaster claimed to have received divine revelation from a being named Voluh Manah that made him aware of how his people had formed certain mistaken ideas about the true nature of the divine world and cosmic order. Zoroaster explained to the Indo-Iranians that there was only one benevolent god, Ahura Mazda. However, he did not claim that the other worshipped deities did not exist. Instead, Zoroaster explained that these other entities were not gods but special beings created by Ahura Mazda to assist humankind and aid in the battle against evil. He called these beings, which he claimed were still worthy of human adoration, *yazatas* (which, appropriately enough, means "worthy of adoration"). In addition, Zoroaster claimed that a race of beings called daevas were the servants of the evil Angra Mainyu.

Even though the word had not yet been created, Zoroaster was saying that the *yazatas* were "angels." In fact, the writings about the angelic entities in the book of Enoch are believed to have been heavily influenced by this idea in Zoroastrianism.

Another possible influence Zoroaster had on the ancient writings of Judaism, both canonical and apocryphal, has to do with the portrayal of God on a divine throne surrounded by angels. Zoroastrian texts describe Ahura Mazda as ruler of the Domain of Light, in which he sat upon his heavenly throne while wearing the sky above as robes. As in Judaism, Ahura Mazda's throne is surrounded by seven of his created beings (much as the Judeo-Christian God's throne is often written to be surrounded by seven angels).

Since the dawn of creation, these brothers of Light and Dark have waged war for the lives and souls of humankind. Eventually, of course, every war must come to an end. Usually, this means someone wins . . . and someone loses. Zoroastrianism bears a number of striking similarities to the Judeo-Christian ideas regarding the Apocalypse. And it is generally believed that many of the apocalyptic concepts of early Judaism were heavily influenced by those found in Zoroastrianism.

The Zoroastrian Apocalypse portrays a final war between Ahura Mazda (alongside his *yazatas*) and Angra Mainyu (with his daevas), just like the final showdowns between the forces of good and evil that one finds in Judaism and Christianity (as well as many other world religions). Eventually, Zoroastrianism teaches, Ahura Mazda and his *yazatas* will defeat Angra Mainyu and his minions in a final and terrible battle that will more or less hit the restart button on existence. The physical world will be destroyed, but those who have remained loyal to the ways of Ahura Mazda will be rewarded with eternity in the Paradise of Light.

Perhaps the multitude of close similarities between the Zoroastrian and Judeo-Christian Apocalypses explains why neither Ahura Mazda nor Zoroaster were included in the roll call of pre-Christian gods who assembled in "Hammer of the Gods" (5-19).

THE HAMMER OF THE PRE-CHRISTIAN GODS

In "Hammer of the Gods," the angels and Lucifer find themselves at odds with a number of powerful deities from across the globe. This episode introduced viewers to gods from various pre-Christian religions as well as to the unique apocalyptic concepts attached to each. Dean and Sam unknowingly stumble into a hotel that the gods have renovated in order to trap the Winchester brothers, the chosen vessels for both Michael and Lucifer, and use them as leverage against their Judeo-Christian adversaries.

THE ELYSIAN FIELDS

The first clue that should have told the Winchesters something wasn't quite right with the hotel was the name of the place: Elysian Fields. This is a reference to the green fields of Elysium, which in Greek mythology is said to be the dwelling place of those dead who were blessed and/or brave. Elysium was far different from the dark Greek underworld of the dead and home to the death god Hades where those who died violently or did not receive proper burial rights found themselves. In many respects, Elysium is about as close as one can get in finding a Greek equivalent of the Judeo-Christian concept of Heaven.

Interestingly enough, the word *Elysium* originally referred to a person or thing that had been struck by lightning. Since lightning was the tool of the mighty Zeus, lord of the Olympian pantheon, this may have been a way of saying that those who inhabit Elysium have been "touched by Zeus." As with the underworld ruled by Hades, the Greeks considered Elysium to be a very real place that had its own geographical location. The Greeks believed that the world was encircled by an enormous river called Oceanus, which would have been located at the planetary equator. The ancient Greeks were ahead of the learning curve in that they believed the world was round (unlike what certain wildly inaccurate history books would have you believe). Greek myths commonly state that Elysium could be found on the farthest western banks of the river Oceanus.

Oceanus was created during the time of the Titans, which were giant, powerful, and often violent creatures that existed before the Greek gods. Most of them were destroyed by Zeus and his fellow Olympians. So the river Oceanus was not just a body of water but a living, breathing, sentient entity, and it is said to be the son of the Greek creation gods Uranus and Gaia. Oceanus is, in turn, the father of all sea nymphs, a race of beautiful female demigoddesses who often acted as the consorts of both gods and heroes alike.

Since Elysium was not located *in* Oceanus but on its farthest western banks, this would basically mean that Elysium was located on the "far side of the world"—a place that in ancient times was altogether unreachable, even for the most skilled of Greek sailors. One could not reach Elysium by traditional means of travel, making it different from the underworld where Greek heroes such as Odysseus were said to have traveled.

Elysium also had another sharp contrast when compared to the underworld—those who inhabit its fields are not spirits. At the moment of death, those chosen to dwell in Elysium were transported there in their own physical (and, presumably, now immortal) bodies. This idea, as you will see later on in this chapter, bears some similarities to the Teutonic concept of Valhalla, where the brave entertain themselves by slaughtering each other in daily combat, only to be healed and resurrected in its grand Mead Hall. Those who dwell in Hades do not have bodies to inhabit, and most Greek myths depict the inhabitants of the Necropolis (a Greek word meaning "city of the dead," sometimes used to refer to the realm of the death god Hades) as sad and wandering shades.

While there are a number of different mythical portrayals of Elysium, the most widely accepted descriptions come from two prominent ancient Greek authors—Homer and Hesiod. Homer described Elysium as a lush green landscape where the weather was always perfect. Homer's Elysium is a land without snow, storms, or rain (and yet it is thick with vegetation) and is the dwelling place of such Greek heroes as King Menelaus. He also claimed the inhabitants lived in physical bodies yet could not die. The land was kept in order by a ruler, King Rhadamanthus.

Hesiod described Elysium as fields found on the Islands of the Blessed. His portrayal of Elysium was similar to Homer's. However, Hesiod claimed that it was ruled by the slain Titan known as Kronos (father of both Zeus and Poseidon, not only the two most powerful Olympian gods but also the ones who slew him) and that Rhadamanthus simply maintained the order of the island in the service of Kronos.

As already stated, even half-god heroes could not reach the distant shores of Elysium under their own steam. For that, they needed the help of a psychopomp, which is somewhat like a divine guide responsible for leading souls to the afterlife (if you just thought "Reaper," give yourself a pat on the back). In Greek myth, one was ushered to an afterlife in either Hades or Elysium by the swiftest member of the Greco-Roman pantheon—Mercury (first known to the Greeks as Hermes).

MERCURY: CONCIERGE OF ELYSIAN FIELDS

I'm quick.

—MERCURY, "HAMMER OF THE GODS" (5-19)

Once you know a bit more about the Elysian Fields, it begins to make sense that Mercury would be running the show (behind the scenes, at least). After all, if Elysium was a hotel, then Mercury would certainly be the one manning the front desk. Even during his earlier Greek portrayals, Mercury was given the role of psychopomp and led the spirits of the chosen dead to the underworld realm of Hades or took them to be physically resurrected in the paradise of Elysium.

As with many of the Olympian gods, Mercury is a son of Zeus. Aside from being a psychopomp, Mercury's second primary duty is as messenger/courier for the Olympian gods. He appears in a very large number of Greco-Roman myths, often bringing messages or gifts (such as special/magical weapons, armor, or items) to heroes from the gods who favor them. He also delivers commands to lesser deities or demigods from their leader, Zeus/Jupiter. For example, the Greek hero Odysseus was trapped on an island for seven years by the sea nymph Calypso, who kept him as a lover and refused to allow him to return to his wife, son, and kingdom in Ithaca. Odysseus is finally freed when Mercury arrives and delivers the orders of Zeus to Calypso that say she must free the hero.

Most of Mercury's duties are related to service, which may explain why he is portrayed in *Supernatural* as the one doing all of the "grunt work."

RAGNARÖK: THE PRE-CHRISTIAN APOCALYPSE OF NORTHERN EUROPE

I don't know what everybody's getting so worked up about. This is just a couple of angels having a slap fight. It's no Armageddon. Everybody knows that when the world comes to an end the great serpent Jormungandr rises up, and I myself will be eaten by a big wolf.

—ODIN, "HAMMER OF THE GODS" (5-19)

In "Hammer of the Gods," the apocalyptic events that Odin describes are from myths of the Norse tradition. He is talking about Ragnarök, which is the Norse version of the Apocalypse. The Norse believed that the universe was held together by a cosmic tree called Yggsdrasil. As with most creation stories, the Norse primal myth has a tree involved. That's right, the Judeo-Christian Tree of Knowledge of Good and Evil isn't the only tree in primal mythology. In fact, there's a multitude of such trees.

Yggsdrasil is an enormous tree (said to be an ash) that grows throughout all levels of existence, connecting them all together. From roots to top, Yggsdrasil connects these realms in the following order:

Nifelheim—Found at Yggsdrasil's roots, Nifelheim is an underworld realm that is ruled by Hel, goddess of death. Some myths also say that the Three Daughters of Jotunheim reside here. The Jotunheim are an ancient race of giants, and these three daughters are the Norse equivalent of the Greek Fates. It is the Three Daughters of Jotunheim who are responsible for all suffering and misfortune in the world. Norse tradition also states that, until the arrival of these fates, the gods were content, kind, and productive.

Midgarth (also spelled Midgard or Middengard)—This area is located at the base of Yggsdrasil's immense trunk. It is the realm of Middle Earth (yes, this is where Tolkien took the name for *The Lord of the Rings* and other books), and it is the land inhabited by human beings and animals.

Utgard—Located in the branches of Yggsdrasil, this is the land of elves and giants.

Asgard—Resting on the top of Yggsdrasil, this is the realm of the Aesir gods. Asgard should not be misinterpreted as the Norse equivalent of a Heaven. The Norse idea of Heaven is a place called Valhalla, ruled over by the most popular god of their mythical tradition—Odin.

Everything that lives must one day die, and even the mighty tree Yggsdrasil is not exempt from this absolute rule of existence. When Ragnarök finally occurs, every member of the Norse pantheon, the Aesir, will have to face an equally powerful being in a final battle. This meeting of such powerful opposing forces will result in mutual death for both sides, kind of like a rhino the size of a planet charging an equally sized elephant. No one survives Ragnarök, not even the powerful Aesir, and certainly not the human race they helped to create.

ODIN: NORSE GOD OF . . . WELL . . . JUST ABOUT EVERYTHING

> Watch your mouth when you talk to me, boy!
> —ODIN, "HAMMER OF THE GODS" (5-19)

In the oldest Norse traditions, the chief god was Tyr (also known as Thor). When Odin (which has alternative spellings such as

Woden, Wotan, or Votan) was introduced to the Norse tradition, he quickly became the most popular god in the Norse pantheon and eventually replaced Tyr in status. The war-hammer-wielding Tyr eventually came to be portrayed as one of Odin's sons.

Odin's popularity led him to be seen as a god of just about every ability, trade, and trait that the Norse valued. The Norse considered Odin to be the wisest being in existence, both all-knowing and all-seeing. Among other things, Odin is the Norse god of war and battle, death, strategy, fatherhood, wisdom, knowledge, wealth, and poetry. He is also the god of mead, a potent wine of fermented honey and the alcoholic beverage of choice for Norse warriors.

Odin defies the usual mythological categories of gods. Usually, creators, destroyers, and psychopomps are portrayed by separate entities in polytheistic pantheons. However, Odin is all three. It was Odin (along with his siblings) who fashioned the realm of Midgard. It is also Odin who favors warriors in battle, making him a destroyer god. Last but not least, it is Odin who leads the souls of the brave and valiant dead to paradise. The Norse paradise is a place called Valhalla, where fallen warriors spend their days butchering each other in battle, their evenings drinking in an incredible Mead Hall, and their nights in bed with the most beautiful of maidens. Not a bad way to spend eternity.

Supernatural's portrayal of Odin has a lot in common with his mythical descriptions. Odin is often physically portrayed in myths as a man of middle age. This was seen as an age of great wisdom at the time, because very few men survived to see the age of twenty. In art he is often shown sitting in the silver halls of Valhalla, on his throne called Hlidskialf. He has another throne located in the realm of Asgard, called Gladsheim, where he conducts meetings with the other Aesir gods. Similar to Zeus/Jupiter in the Greco-Roman pantheon, Odin is the lord of the Aesir (and pretty much the rest of the Norse pantheon). His hair is long and curly, and his chin is adorned with a long gray beard. His clothing is usually gray, and over his apparel he often wears a hooded blue cloak. His face or eyes are often concealed beneath the hood of his cloak or under an extremely wide-brimmed hat. On his arm is Draupnir, an arm ring that provides endless wealth to the wearer. In his hand he grips the spear named Gungnir, "Unwavering," so named because it is endowed with a magical enchantment that causes it to always hit the intended target. The spear Gungnir was created by the members of a dwarf craftsman guild called the Sons of Ivaldi.

Odin's most coveted tools, however, are absent from his portrayal in *Supernatural*—a pair of black ravens. One of the two ravens sits on either of his shoulders. These blackbirds give Odin a strategic edge above any other being in existence. One raven is called Hugin (Thought) and the other Munin (Memory). These two birds can whisper into Odin's ears from their shoulder perches, not just in the form of words, but in thoughts, images, and memories as well, and can act as nearly infallible advisers in any situation. The first raven of Odin, Hugin, always speaks the truth into Odin's ear. This means that if Odin is being tricked, lied to, or otherwise deceived, Hugin will allow him to know the truth. Odin's second raven, Munin, allows Odin to recall any memory with perfect accuracy, and not just his own memories but those of others as well. This means that Odin has access to any memory in existence. This allows him to understand the opinions, emotions, and points of view of others like no other Aesir.

Considering his impressive résumé, it is somewhat saddening

to think of how easily Odin was taken out by Lucifer. It appears that he won't be eaten by a giant wolf, after all.

Speaking of which, that "big wolf" is called Fenrir, and he is one mean, scary pooch (kind of like Crowley's hellhound on steroids). In the final battles of Ragnarök, Odin and Fenrir will clash in battle. Odin will eventually be devoured, but Fenrir will not emerge victorious. The monstrous wolf will be killed in his attempt to swallow the powerful Odin. Fenrir, as with many other troublesome figures in the Norse tradition, is the offspring of the most problematic god among the Aesir—a trickster named Loki.

LOKI (AKA GABRIEL: PART 2)

You think I'd give Kali my real sword? That thing can kill me.
—LOKI/GABRIEL, "HAMMER OF THE GODS" (5-19)

Okay, technically speaking, the Norse god Loki is not a character on *Supernatural*. In "Hammer of the Gods" (5-19) the figure that the pre-Christian gods refer to as Loki is in actuality the archangel Gabriel. Loki is, however, the name of a powerful trickster in the Norse tradition. And the mythical tradition related to this figure offers some insight into why Gabriel chose Loki as his new identity.

While Loki is considered the brother of Odin in the Norse tradition, their relationship has more to do with oath than blood. Loki is actually a son of giants from Jotunheim, the giant Farbauti and giantess Laufey. In many respects, giants in the Norse tradition act similarly to demons in the myths of Judeo-Christianity. One might say that the relationship between Odin and Loki bears some similarities to that of the archangel Michael and his rebellious brother Lucifer.

The Aesir gods treated Loki as one of their own, despite his parentage, though they often had issues with his troublesome nature. Like most tricksters (including Gabriel) Loki can change his shape, including his sex. Despite the fact that he can often be a serious pain in the neck, he is valued by the Aesir because of his partial responsibility in regaining a very special war hammer belonging to Odin's son Tyr. He also once rebuilt the damaged walls of Asgard. When one considers the fact that he was responsible for damaging the walls in the first place, however, this doesn't seem quite so noble. From his early inclusion in the Aesir to his later depictions, Loki's behavior becomes increasingly severe in nature. He goes from being a playful trickster to a more violent and demonic figure. His actions go from annoying, to troublesome but relatively harmless, to downright malicious and dangerous.

The Aesir finally lose patience with Loki's pranks when one of them results in the death of a fellow, and especially beloved, Aesir named Baldur. Baldur's death sets in motion the first stages of Ragnarök, which will take thousands of years before reaching a violent conclusion. For this transgression, Loki was taken to the dark realm of Nifelheim (somewhat comparable to Lucifer's imprisonment in Hell) and chained to three enormous boulders: one boulder was chained across and under his shoulders, one boulder was chained under his knees, and the third and final boulder was chained to his groin. The final boulder pretty much seals the deal. After all, it would be pretty hard to go anywhere when you have an enormous chunk of rock chained to your junk.

The Norse mythical tradition also states that Loki won't stay chained up forever. In the final violent days of Ragnarök, Loki will break free from his chains and lead the giants into battle against the remaining members of the Aesir (again, similar to the battles between angels and demons in the Judeo-Christian traditions).

> Surprise, surprise. The trickster has tricked us.
>
> —KALI, "HAMMER OF THE GODS" (5-19)

BALDUR'S DEATH AND RAGNARÖK

> LOKI/GABRIEL: Baldur? Seriously?
> KALI: Baldur's uncomplicated.
>
> —GABRIEL AND KALI, "HAMMER OF THE GODS" (5-19)

Baldur is the Norse god of light and joy. He is also a twin, and he and his brother Hodur (also spelled Hodr or Holdur) are the sons of Odin and Freya (sometimes spelled Frigga), Odin's wife as well as the patron goddess of marriage and queen of the Aesir. Both are said to be very handsome, but Hodur, unlike Baldur, was born blind. This comes into play later on.

To protect her beloved sons, Freya obtains oaths from all plants and trees that they will never bring harm to her sons. The only plant she fails to obtain this oath from is the mistletoe. Some say this is because mistletoe was not considered suitable for making weapons, while others claim that it has something to do with the wood's magical properties.

Loki finds out about Baldur's vulnerability and just cannot help himself: he constructs a dart out of mistletoe and convinces the blind Hodur to unknowingly throw it in the direction of his twin brother Baldur (Loki stood behind Hodur and told him where to throw). The unsuspecting Baldur was struck by the dart and killed. Needless to say, the Aesir were pissed (especially Freya).

Freya gets Hel, goddess of the underworld, to agree to release Baldur from the afterlife if everyone in existence weeps for him. Loki thwarts this, however, and hides out by disguising himself as an old woman giant. He refuses to shed tears for Baldur and so Hel does not release the fallen Aesir. In the end, Odin himself has to go into the underworld to retrieve his dead son.

While the Norse story, from the *Edda*, is the most popular version of Baldur's death, the Scandinavian tradition has an alternative version in the text called *Saxo Grammaticus*. In this version Hodur is directly responsible for his twin's death. Hodur slays Baldur with a magic sword during a quarrel the twins get into over a beautiful maiden named Nanna.

Considering Baldur's background of death and resurrection, perhaps it only makes sense that Kali would find him attractive (though she seems to still hold a flame in her heart for Loki/Gabriel). After all, she is a goddess of death, illness, and destruction, with a well-known tendency to kill her lovers. The two seem to fit together . . . though, admittedly, in a twisted sort of way.

THE KALI YUGA OF HINDU DHARMA

The Hindu Dharma religion, of which the goddess Kali and god Ganesh are part, has its own take on the Apocalypse. The concept divides existence into separate ages, called yugas. Hindu belief states that existence occurs in cycles, and that each cycle plays out in a series of these yugas. This is not the first cycle of existence, and it is unlikely to be the last. Each existence cycle, however, ends with what is called (in this current existence cycle, at least—it is probably given different names in other cycles, past and future) the Kali Yuga. Roughly translated, this means the "Age of Kali," but it would be more accurately interpreted to mean the "Age of Dark/ Death/Destruction." The name for the age is fitting, since Hindu belief states that Kali has a role to play in the end of all things.

The start of the Kali Yuga is traditionally marked in the Hindu mythical tradition by the death of Krishna, the eighth avatar of the supreme god Vishnu. Vishnu is one of the three supreme gods who make up the godhead: Brahma (creator god), Vishnu (sustainer god), and Shiva (destroyer god). Vishnu often took human form by incarnating himself into infants at times when the world needed his help. These human forms are called avatars.

Krishna's death may mark the start of the Kali Yuga, but he is not the last avatar of Vishnu. Hindu Dharma believes that there will be ten total avatars. The ninth avatar was Buddha, though this is not a belief commonly shared by Buddhists. The tenth and final avatar of Vishnu is referred to by the name Kalki (not to be confused with the goddess Kali). The appearance of Kalki will lead to the destruction of all evil on Earth. In the Hindu belief, "evil" is commonly linked to the human desires caused by physical existence, the root to all suffering, as explained by the ninth avatar Buddha.

The prophecy states that Kalki will appear at the end of the Kali Yuga. He will descend from the sky, with such size and grandeur that he will be visible to all on the Earth. Interestingly enough, the prophecy also states that Kalki will appear riding a white horse and wielding a fiery sword. Sound familiar? It should, since a similar description exists for one of the Four Horsemen of the Apocalypse in Christianity's book of Revelation. Aside from the prophecy, there are no myths about Kalki, since he has not yet appeared on Earth. *What* Kalki is going to do (kick off the obliteration of physical existence, most likely) is more important than *how* he is going to do it. When he does appear, there will be an amazing tale to tell. Too bad there won't be anyone around to tell about it.

KALI: THE DARK ONE

You're sweet . . . I hate sweet.

—KALI, "HAMMER OF THE GODS" (5-19)

In the Hindu Dharma mythos, the goddess Kali is known as the Black One. She is one scary chick, giving even Lilith a run for her money. As discussed in chapter 8, some myth scholars have theorized that Kali may have even been created based on myths that reached India from nearby Mesopotamia. This is mainly speculation based on the fact that one of Lilith's early Sumerian names was Kal.

Kali's skin is pitch-black. Long, curved, and often blood-drenched fangs protrude out of her mouth. Curving down from between her dark lips is a long, bloodred tongue. Around her neck she wears a necklace of human skulls. In art, rivers of blood are often shown flowing away from her.

SUPERNATURAL FACTS

In one "Hammer of the Gods" (5-19) scene, Baldur is shown helping Kali put on a necklace. This act may have been done as a reference to Kali's necklace of skulls in her mythological depictions.

Kali is said to live at the top of Mount Vindhya in India, from where she observes our suffering. Nothing delights Kali more than death, sickness, and misery. Some Hindu Dharma myths state that Kali's malevolent nature stems from the fact that she was once a human baby who was killed by a parent or other relative, making her the first victim of infanticide. Since she was the first mortal baby to be murdered, her soul ascended into the heavens and took on the form of a wrathful goddess of death, destruction, and pestilence.

Kali is a harbinger of death, but she has a role to play in the cycle of existence. After all, it's not called the Kali Yuga for nothing. She is a consort of Shiva, the Hindu Lord of Death, and at times, she is portrayed as his wife. Some myths claim that only Shiva had the strength to tame her reckless and violent nature and take her as a lover. However, at the climax of the Kali Yuga, Shiva will meet his end at Kali's hands.

Since Shiva is also the Hindu Dharma god of destruction, it is only fitting that Kali would be closely associated with him. However, his true wife is said to be the beautiful and merciful goddess Shakti. He and Shakti become one to create a somewhat androgynous form of what is commonly called the Dancing Shiva, or Shiva Nataraja.

When Kali and Shiva danced, they did not join but instead brought terrible destruction upon the Earth. When they dance again, the planet will not survive. Kali will draw her blade and stab Shiva. She will then stand upon his corpse. With the "death of death," so to speak, all that will remain is the dark void of oblivion. Even Kali will one day cease to be, consumed by her own vast darkness.

GANESH: "FULL-ON BABAR"

SAM: An elephant?
DEAN: Yeah.
SAM: Like, an elephant?
DEAN: Like full-on Babar.
—SAM AND DEAN, "HAMMER OF THE GODS" (5-19)

The name of the Hindu Dharma god Ganesh (also spelled Ganesa or Ganesha, sometimes Ganapati) is commonly translated as "Lord of Hosts." In the Hindu mythical tradition, the elephant-headed Ganesh is the god of wisdom, good judgment, and learning. Ganesh is also the "remover of obstacles." Because of these attributes, Ganesh is often worshipped or consulted by people who are experiencing times of difficulty. The same goes for merchants seeking prudence in their financial dealings.

Ganesh has the head of an elephant, which is symbolic of his ability to tear down any obstacle. After all, a good-sized elephant at full charge is capable of knocking down just about anything in its path. While his head may be symbolic of his abilities, he does literally have the head of an elephant. In fact, many of the myths about Ganesh have to do with his elephant head.

Ganesh is the son of Shiva and the devi (a lower-order deity) named Parvati. When he was born, Parvati was so proud that she rushed to show the infant to his father. Apparently, Shiva was none too happy about his newborn son, and the wrathful god shot such a terrible glance at the infant that it reduced Ganesh's entire head to ashes. Parvati took her headless baby to the creator god Brahma, who told her that she could save the child if she replaced his lost head with the first one she could find. Needless to say, the first head she found belonged to an elephant. In an interesting turn, this gave Ganesh great wisdom. After all, it has long been known that real elephants possess remarkable memory skills. Apparently, even the ancient Hindi culture was aware of this.

Another myth gives a different version of the story. This one claims that his headlessness occurred when he was older. According to this version, Shiva once wished to enter Parvati's bathing chamber and found the entrance blocked by Ganesh. When Ganesh refused to allow Shiva to pass, the angry god drew his blade and took off his son's head. Realizing that Parvati would be furious if he left their son headless, Shiva replaced the lost head with an elephant's.

This isn't the only time Ganesh would be maimed as a result of getting in someone's way. Ganesh is often portrayed with tusks, one of which appears to have been cut. According to the Hindu epic *Ramayana* (Power of Rama), the prince Rama (who was the seventh avatar of Vishnu) once visited Shiva as the destructive god was napping. Ganesh, perhaps not realizing that he was dealing with Vishnu incarnate, attempted to block Rama from entering the room. Rama tossed an ax, which belonged to Shiva, at Ganesh's head. Ganesh, recognizing his father's weapon, allowed it to sever one of his tusks (or perhaps he just couldn't get out of the way in time).

ZAO CHEN AND THE WORLD TURTLE

> ODIN: Because your beliefs are so much more realistic? The whole world's getting carried around on the back of a giant turtle? Ha! Give me a break!
>
> ZAO CHEN: Don't mock my World Turtle!
>
> —ZAO CHEN, "HAMMER OF THE GODS" (5-19)

Probably the most unusual figure at the table in "Hammer of the Gods" is the Chinese kitchen god Zao Chen. His name has a ton of alternative spellings (Tsao Chen, Tsao Shen, and Zao Kung, to name only a few). As a kitchen god, Zao Chen is the god of the stove or hearth. This would explain why the Zao Chen in *Supernatural* spent so much time in the hotel kitchen. As Dean put it, upon finding a soup pot full of dismembered body parts, "Please be tomato soup, please be tomato soup . . . great . . . motel hell."

Interestingly enough, Zao Chen is the most widely worshipped deity of the Chinese pantheon. His worshippers come from all social and financial classes. His ceremonies are observed by both young and old, rich and poor, educated and uneducated. After all, everybody's got to eat. Zao Chen spends the majority of his time on Earth watching over the kitchens of the world. Once a year, however, he returns to the heavenly realm of the Jade Emperor so that he can deliver his reports about the misdeeds that have occurred in the kitchens of mortals. Ceremonies are held during this time, in which sweet treats are given as offerings (or bribes?) to Zao Chen. He is said to be unable to resist such treats. Actually, the idea is that Zao Chen's lips will get stuck together by the sticky treats and prevent him from making any bad reports. Depending on where in China the ceremony is held, his departure is on the twenty-third, twenty-fourth, or twenty-sixth day of the Eleventh Moon. His trip lasts roughly a week, and his return to Earth is marked by another round of sweet offerings.

Basically, Zao Chen is tasked with enforcing certain rules related to the preparation of food. These rules are similar in nature to the Jewish food restrictions from the Old Testament. They have to do mainly with hygiene and decency. It's an extremely long list, but here is a sampling of his rules:

- No one may be naked in front of a stove.

- Living creatures may not be slaughtered in the kitchen.

- No obscenities or lewd song may be uttered in front of a stove.

- Old papers, animal bones, discarded rags, brooms, or hair must not be burned in the stove.

- No living (not yet slaughtered) animal may ever be put in a pot or on the stove.

Breaking the above rules will bring bad reports from Zao Chen. Repeat offenses may even bring down his direct wrath. For example, if ants, insects, or rodents are allowed to make nests in a stove (caused by neglect in cleaning), Zao Chen is said to become especially angry. His anger may manifest in the form of digestive problems or accidents in the kitchen. For example, he might give you a nudge while you're cutting carrots and make you take off your own finger.

But what about the World Turtle that, when teased by Odin, made Zao Chen become so irate? The World Turtle is certainly a part of the Chinese mythos; however, it has no direct association with Zao Chen. The Chinese mythical tradition explains that a creator goddess named Nu Gua needed a way to prop up the heavens over Earth after the mountain that had originally done so (Buzhou Mountain) was damaged. To do this, she used legs of an enormous sea turtle that had enveloped all realms (called Ao, pronounced similar to "ow," or a quick form of "ah-oh"). The flat underbelly of Ao the World Turtle is the flat ground upon which humans walk. Its domed shell is the sky above.

BARON SAMEDI: HOODOO-VOODOO LORD OF DEATH

Baron Samedi can be broadly classified as a voodoo death god. However, this classification seems to create a mistaken impression. Originally, Baron Samedi is believed to have been referred to by the name Ghede. At some point, though, the name was changed to the French Samedi, or "Saturday." Some scholars have theorized that indentured servants from Ireland, who worked the Caribbean sugar plantations alongside African slaves, may have integrated their concept of Samhain into the Haitian voodoo death god. When one considers that Samhain refers to a specific time of year and is not the name of an actual deity (see chapter 3 for more on Samhain), this hypothesis seems unlikely.

In voodoo, Baron Samedi is one of the *loa* (a powerful, almost godlike spirit). He is sometimes referred to by the nickname "the Great Boss," and he is the patron *loa* spirit of the dead. Just like his portrayal in *Supernatural*, Baron Samedi likes to smoke cigars and is usually shown with one in his hand or mouth. He is also a rather snappy dresser.

Baron Samedi is often shown wearing a black tuxedo, or an undertaker's suit as if "dressed for a funeral." His face is often a skull or at least skull-like (for example, a human face painted to resemble a skull). Sometimes he looks like a man whose upper face is painted like a skull. On Baron Samedi's skull-like head usually rests a high top hat, and in his hand he twirls a long cane usually cut from a dark wood, such as ebony. It is not uncommon for his cane to be adorned by a silver skull at the handle.

Baron Samedi commonly manifests before people in one of two forms, depending on the reason he is invoked. The first is for his role as a psychopomp, in which he is called Baron-La-Croix (Baron Cross). In this form, Baron Samedi stands at the crossroads between the land of the living and the realm of the dead. His second form is related to his role as the guardian of cemeteries, graveyards, and burial plots. This form is called Baron Cimetière (Baron of the Cemeteries). Baron Samedi has a great dislike for grave robbers and those who desecrate corpses. And this dislike includes voodoo *houngans* (a term for voodoo/hoodoo priests) who have gone into the dark practice of raising zombies. Such *houngans* must make proper rites and offerings to Baron Samedi to enter safely. Usually, tobacco will do (especially cigars). Some believe these separate portrayals are actually independent *loa* who serve or are related to Baron Samedi. When it comes to the *loa*, as with demons, space and separation are blurred concepts. One *loa* can become several, or multiple *loa* can join to become a single *loa*. This makes them hard to count.

Unfortunately for the pre-Christian figures portrayed in "Hammer of the Gods," Lucifer showed up and wasted all of them. It looked like the Judeo-Christian Apocalypse was going to happen after all. But Lucifer didn't count on Dean Winchester—armed with nothing but a bitchin' ride, a Def Leppard tape, a "GED and a 'give 'em hell' attitude"—throwing a monkey wrench into his little "slap fight" with Michael. For now, Armageddon has been averted. Unfortunately, only God knows what the next chapter of the Winchester Gospel will hold—and he isn't talking.

≡ 10 ≡

THE WINCHESTER GOSPEL— *SUPERNATURAL* AS MYTH

In addition to the lore used to create the show that is *Supernatural*, the series also makes use of a number of elements from mythology. The show integrates many mythological themes and concepts, from Judeo-Christian lore to mythological archetypes related to feuding brothers, from religious and philosophical concepts about the nature of reality to metaphors for father/son and human/god relationships. In a way, the show *Supernatural* is very much a modern mythos in and of itself.

THE FEUDING BROTHERS ARCHETYPE

No one dicks with Michael but me.

—LUCIFER, "SWAN SONG" (5-22)

Brothers fight . . . it's pretty much a universal truth. So perhaps it is no surprise that Michael and Lucifer (or Sam and Dean) aren't the only feuding brothers in mythology. As already discussed, the Norse god Odin was often at odds with his troublesome brother Loki. From the Norse to the Romans, from ancient Egypt to Mesopotamia, nearly every mythological tradition has a story about brothers who fight, often ending with one brother killing the other.

Although Sam and Dean Winchester often have their fights, as brothers will, they love each other. However, even Dean Winchester has had moments when he believed that he might have to kill his brother Sam one day if, as John Winchester long feared, the demon blood given him by Azazel finally caused Sam to "go dark side," as they often put it on the show.

FOUNDERS OF ROME: ROMULUS AND REMUS

When it comes to the archetype of feuding brothers, one of the most well-known tales in Western mythology is that of Romulus and Remus, creators of the great city of Rome. These twin brothers are said to have been the demigod sons of Mars, the god of war, and Rhea Silvia, a Vestal Virgin (a celibate-bound priestess of the goddess Vesta/Hestia). When they were but infants, the Tiber River flooded and caused Romulus and Remus to be set adrift by the torrent in a small vessel. Eventually, they washed ashore near the site of what would one day be Rome. The babies were found by an enormous she-wolf, who guarded and suckled them until they were old enough to fight and fend for themselves.

As a result, the boys grew up tough, strong, and more than a bit wild.

Once they had grown into men, the brothers decided to set about the task of building their own city. Remus built the interior while Romulus built the walls. When their work was through, Romulus marveled at his work and thought that no one could breach the mighty walls he'd built for their new city. Remus, however, being the typical brother he was, took a running start at the walls and cleared them in a single bound (brothers just can't help but mess with each other, can they?).

Seeing Remus clear his beloved walls, Romulus grew enraged. He and Remus soon got into a quarrel (some versions say they began bickering about whose contribution to the city was the greater of the two). Brotherly bickering soon turned to shoving, and shoving soon turned to blows. The situation escalated until the half-god twins were engaged in a furious life-and-death battle, and during the violence Romulus killed Remus.

FEUDING GODS OF EGYPT: SET AND OSIRIS

Even the ancient Egyptians were well aware of how brothers tend to fight, especially when one is good and the other is evil. In the mythos of ancient Egypt, the "feuding brothers" archetype is personified by the benevolent god Osiris and his cruel and wicked brother Set (sometimes spelled Seth). One story about these two is among the oldest and most beloved ancient Egyptian myths. The story was not written down until Roman times. A Roman named Plutarch wrote the story down, and in his writings claimed that it was the key to understanding the mysteries surrounding the Egyptian religious beliefs. The imagery of this story, however, has been found in ancient inscriptions on the walls of tombs and temples, as well as in the hieroglyphics of Books of the Dead. These "books" are actually tiny papyrus scrolls that were placed in sarcophagi alongside mummies and were meant to serve as guides to help the souls of the deceased navigate their way through the underworld and into the paradise of the afterlife.

This particular story tells of how Osiris, an ancient god-king of Egypt, was killed by his evil brother Set. During a rather wild party, Osiris was deceived into lying down in a coffin by Set. Once inside, seventy-two of Set's conspirators immediately slammed down the heavy lid and nailed it shut. They carried the coffin to the shores of the Nile River, placed it on a barge, and set it adrift. The barge floated up the Nile until it finally came ashore by a lavish palace near Abydos. Shortly after hitting land, the intoxicating smell of the coffin attracted a throng of royal servants from the nearby palace. The servants pulled the coffin out, dragged it into the palace courtyard, and stood it on its end. In a surprisingly short time, an Erica tree sprang up around the coffin until it was fully engulfed.

It didn't take long for Osiris's wife (and sister), Isis, to realize that her husband had gone missing. She went looking for him and eventually made her way to the Erica tree near Abydos. The goddess disguised herself as a mortal and, for a short time, worked in the palace as nursemaid to the princess of Abydos, who had just given birth to a baby boy. Isis even tried to grant immortality to the infant son of the princess of Abydos using a fire spell. When the princess walked in on this and saw her baby playing with his toys while engulfed in flames, she understandably freaked out. The princess let out a loud shriek, breaking Isis's concentration along with the immortality fire spell. Isis revealed her true radiant form, informed the princess that she just cost her baby boy the gift of immortality, and demanded to be allowed to take her husband's coffin from the tree. The princess, of course, conceded to Isis's wishes.

Isis carved the coffin out of the trunk of the Erica tree, put it once again on a barge in the Nile, and floated it back toward home until midnight. At this auspicious hour, Isis spread out her wings and hovered above the corpse of her dead husband/brother. She brought Osiris back to life by flapping her powerful wings over his corpse. The two made love and she gave birth to a new god— Horus, a hawk-headed figure who later became a popular god in the Egyptian pantheon. Isis, according to a number of depictions in ancient art, took the baby god Horus to the marshes and hid him in the reeds so that Set would not harm him.

Set became furious when he heard of his brother's resurrection. With the help of his seventy-two conspirators, he managed to hunt down Osiris with the intention of killing his brother again, hopefully for good this time. Set and his men fell upon Osiris in an ambush and chopped him into many pieces. They then scattered the dismembered pieces all over the land of Egypt so that he could not be resurrected by Isis. One legend says that in every spot where a piece of Osiris's body fell, a temple was erected to honor him.

Horus took to the skies and sought out every piece of his father's body. He succeeded in finding every piece but the one that mattered most, his "wedding tackle" (pun intended), because it had been swallowed by a fish. He and Isis fashioned a wooden phallus to replace it, and Osiris was once again raised from the dead (more or less intact). This time, he was reborn as the Lord of Death and Resurrection. In many of the Egyptian Books of the Dead, Osiris is depicted sitting in his throne room with his sister Nepthys and wife, Isis. Above him sits a row of cobras with their hoods inflated around solar disks. Osiris is also often shown holding a shepherd's hooked staff in one hand and a royal scepter in the other.

On the walls of tombs and temples, Osiris is commonly depicted in his role as Lord of the Staircase. This title refers to the sixth hour of sleep, when the soul was believed to make a nightly journey into the realm of the underworld by way of a magical staircase. In the background of such depictions, Set can often be seen. However, he has been transformed into a black pig and is being driven into the exile of the wilderness as punishment for his crimes. Speaking of brothers who are exiled as punishment for fratricide, our next story brings us to one of the most infamous brotherly quarrels in world mythology.

THE FALL OF THE SONS OF ADAM: CAIN AND ABEL

Just about everyone in the Western world knows the story of Cain and Abel. In fact, this is probably one of the most common mythological associations people make to quarreling brothers. However, in comparison to the relationship between Dean and

Sam, there is one big difference—unlike Dean, Cain refuses to take responsibility for his brother (or anything else).

While many people assume that the only version of the Cain and Abel story comes from the Bible, this is not the case. All versions of the myth agree that Cain was the firstborn son of Adam and Eve. There are some alternative, though admittedly less credible, versions of the myth that have tried to associate Cain with Lilith (see chapter 8). However, there is no legitimate mythical basis for this association.

In the Judeo-Christian version of the myth, Cain was the first person to take a human life. He and Abel go to make offerings to God; Cain's sacrifice is of wheat or grain, and Abel's is from his livestock. As the offerings are burned, the smoke from Abel's sacrificial animal rises to the heavens as a sign that God is pleased with it. The smoke from Cain's offering, however, does not rise, signaling that God has rejected it. Enraged that Abel's offerings have been accepted by God while his own are rejected, Cain flies into a rage and attacks his brother. In his anger, Cain kills Abel.

Realizing what he has done, Cain runs and attempts to hide from the sight of God. The all-seeing God cannot be hidden from, of course, and comes to where Cain is hiding. When God asks Cain where his little brother has gone, Cain makes the now infamous reply, "I am not my brother's keeper" (See? Cain was the "anti-Dean"). God, of course, already knows what Cain has done. As divine punishment for committing the murderous act of fratricide, Cain's head is forever stained with a "mark" by God, and Cain is exiled into the wasteland known as Nod. The meaning of the so-called mark of Cain is a matter of debate. The myth doesn't make the purpose of this mark entirely clear. Some say that the mark of Cain is a badge of shame. Others claim that it instead served to protect him from those who might try to kill him as retribution for killing his brother. Even this second interpretation has two sides, because it is unclear if the mark of Cain only served as a visual warning or if it actively protected him from harm.

There is yet another interpretation of the mark of Cain. In myth Cain is said to have been associated with an ancient Semitic tribe known as the Kenites, who are believed to have worn some form of unique mark upon their foreheads. This may have been the origin of the mark of Cain element of the story. Proponents of this interpretation believe that the myth of Cain and Abel is an allegory for the fall of an ancient agricultural Semitic tribe (in ancient times, most Hebrew tribes were nomadic herders).

In the Muslim version of this "brother versus brother" myth, however, Cain's motivations for killing Abel are even more selfish. You may be thinking, "What could be more selfish than killing your brother for being favored by God?" Well, in this version of the myth Cain and Abel are both born with their own twin sisters. When his children reach marriage age, Adam decides to marry each brother to his twin sister. Cain, however, feels that he is getting the short end of the stick in the deal because Abel's twin sister is far more attractive than his own. Enraged by the knowledge that he would be forced to marry the less attractive of the two sisters, Cain begins throwing stones at Abel. Eventually, one of the stones hits a fatal spot and Abel falls dead.

Also in the Muslim version, Cain is unsure about what to do with his dead brother's corpse until he sees two ravens quarreling. When the fight between the blackbirds is over, one lies dead. The victor raven scrapes a trench into the soil and buries his fallen opponent in it. Seeing this inspires Cain to do the same, and he buries Abel's dead body in the earth. Because of this, Allah curses the Earth for allowing Abel's body to be buried within it. Allah then exiles Cain, along with his twin sister (yes, the "ugly one"), into the land of Nod.

After Cain went into exile, it is said that he created the first city of humankind and fathered a tribe of his own, the Kenites, with his twin sister (for him at least, she was the last woman on Earth). Cain's descendants are said to have been an evil people who developed a number of evil inventions and ideas that accelerated the destruction of humankind—walls and boundaries, units of measurement, laws, and, most evil of all in the view of Hebraic nomadic shepherds, land ownership. These malevolent inventions, the story goes, bound humans to physical possessions and brought about an end to human freedom, which to this day has not been restored.

Most versions agree on how Cain met his end. In an ironic twist of fate, Cain was killed by the hand of one of his own descendents, Lamech, the son of Methushael. Methushael was Cain's great-grandson, the chronology of which suggests that Cain lived for roughly three hundred years.

ANGELIC VESSELS: BLOOD OF THE NEPHILIM?

Certain people, special people, can perceive my true visage. I thought you would be one of them. I was wrong.

—CASTIEL, "LAZARUS RISING" (4-1)

One biblical story that has puzzled Christians for centuries stems from the following passage from the book of Genesis:

> *It came to pass, when men began to multiply across the face of the Earth, and daughters were born to them, that the Sons of God saw the beauty of the daughters of men; and the Sons of God took the wives for themselves, choosing from the daughters of men. Then the Lord said, "My Spirit shall not strive with Man forever, for he is indeed flesh; yet his days shall be one hundred and twenty years."*
>
> —GENESIS 6:1–3

This part of Genesis refers to an event that was drawn out in much greater detail in the book of Enoch. The "Sons of God" were in fact angels who chose to mate with humans. As you read in chapter 3, a number of these angels (such as Azazel) also corrupted humans with new technologies and ideas that allowed them to wage wars and otherwise sped up their self-destruction.

Where there is sex, of course, there are usually children. And the Sons of God who mated with the daughters of men were no different. They gave birth to a race of powerful giants, called Nephilim. This event, which was previously given far more attention in the book of Enoch, is also briefly referred to in the Judeo-Christian Genesis:

> *The Sons of God came in to the daughters of men and bore children. They produced giants* (or, in some translations, Nephilim)

who were on the Earth in those days, and also afterward. Those were the mighty men who were of old, men of renown who were later wiped out by the flood.

—GENESIS 6:4

Now compare the above passages to those from the book of Enoch, which directly associates the birth of the Nephilim with the rebel angels:

And it came to pass in those days when the children of men had multiplied that beautiful and comely daughters were born unto them. And the angels, the children of Heaven, saw and lusted after the daughters of men, and said to one another: "Come, let us choose wives from among the children of men and with them beget children." And Semlazaz, who was their leader, said unto the others, "I fear you all will not indeed agree to commit this deed, and I alone shall have to pay the penalty of a great sin." And they all answered to him: "Let us all swear an oath, and all bind ourselves by mutual imprecations not to abandon our plan but to commit this deed." Then they all swore and bound themselves by mutual imprecations upon it. And they were two-hundred in all; who descended to Earth in the days of Jared on the summit of Mount Hermon . . . And these are the names of their leaders: Semlazaz the leader, Araklba, Kokablel, Tamlel, Ramlel, Danel, Ezeqael, Baraqijal, Azazel, Armaros, Batarel, Zachariel, Samsapael, Satarel, Turel, Jomjael, Sariel.

—BOOK OF ENOCH (ETHIOPIAN VERSION)

The book of Enoch tells of how these fallen angels were cast forever into places of darkness. However, in the writings of the book of Jubilees it is explained that God allowed 10 percent of the Nephilim (and many of the fallen angels) to wander the Earth as disembodied spirits or demons so that they could corrupt the children of men with various temptations until the coming of the Final Judgment.

As for the Nephilim who inhabited the Earth after the fall of their angelic fathers, they quickly became a serious problem for humans. They raped, pillaged, plundered, and destroyed until humans found themselves unable to sustain their own survival. Therefore, God chose to destroy the Nephilim. There is not a full consensus among the texts that discuss the destruction of the Nephilim. Some texts claim that God sent his archangels to destroy them, while others claim that the obliteration of the Nephilim was one of the reasons for the Great Deluge that occurred in the time of Noah.

If some of the Nephilim survived the wrath of God, however, then it would explain why (in the lore of *Supernatural*, at least) certain human bloodlines are suited to act as angelic vessels while others are not. Perhaps the Winchesters are descendents of the Nephilim?

AS IT IS IN HEAVEN, SO MUST IT BE ON EARTH

Why do you think you two are the vessels? Think about it. Michael—the big brother, loyal to an absent father. And

Lucifer—the little brother, rebellious of Daddy's plan. You were born to this, boys! It's your destiny! It was always you! "As it is in Heaven, so must it be on Earth!"

—GABRIEL, "CHANGING CHANNELS" (5-8)

In the above quote, Gabriel isn't just pulling rules out of his keister. This is nearly a direct citation from the biblical book of Matthew 6:10—"Thy Kingdom come, Thy will be done, on Earth as it is in Heaven." This verse makes up part of what is widely known as the Lord's Prayer and has been commonly interpreted to mean that events that transpire on Earth mirror events that occur in Heaven.

When Moses constructed a temple for the Hebrews, he went up the mountain in order to receive revelation from God regarding how this should be done. God gave Moses very specific instructions as to the manner in which the tabernacle's structure was to be built as well as how the contents within it were to be arranged. Later in the anonymously authored New Testament book Epistle to the Hebrews, the meaning behind the circumstances of Moses's construction of this very same temple is addressed in a discussion of the roles of the Hebrew priests within the temple:

They serve at a sanctuary that is a copy and shadow of what is in Heaven. This is why Moses was warned [by God] when he was about to construct the tabernacle: "See to it that you make everything according to the pattern shown you on the mountain."

—HEBREWS 8:5

The exact nature with which the temple needed to be built, along with the above passage from Hebrews, suggests that the temple of the Hebrews was erected in a specific pattern meant to mirror that of God's heavenly temple. While things on Earth might reflect those in Heaven, these reflections are imperfect by comparison to the perfect reality of God's realm. For example, the sacrifices of livestock to God were but imperfect reflections of the sacrifice of the Christ. This idea is also expressed in the Epistle to the Hebrews, as follows:

> *The law is only a shadow of the good things to come—not the realities themselves. For this reason it can never, by the same sacrifices repeated endlessly year after year, make perfect those who draw near in worship. If it could, would not the sacrifices stop? For the worshipers would have been cleansed once and for all, and would no longer have felt guilty for their sins. Those sacrifices are but yearly reminders of sins, because it is impossible for the blood of bulls to take away sins.*
>
> —HEBREWS 10:1–4

The idea that the physical realm imperfectly mirrors a divine realm (Heaven) is in no way exclusive to Christianity.

A similar Heaven-and-Earth concept exists in the Hermetic tradition of philosophy and mysticism, which worships a deity that combines attributes of the Greek god Hermes and the Egyptian god Thoth. The Hermetic philosophers believed that all planes of reality—physical, spiritual, and mental/psychological—exist on top of one another and therefore must reflect one another to an extent. This means that whatever happens on one plane of existence must simultaneously occur, in some form, on the other planes. The Hermetic tradition sees this parallelism as extending across all things. For example, the events that occur throughout the vast universe, the macrocosm, will be mimicked within the microcosm of an individual human or living organism. This Hermetic concept also exists in a number of other magical practices— "as above, so below."

The Greek philosopher Plato expressed a similar idea, well over three hundred years before the coming of Christ, that physical existence was but an imperfect imitation or reflection of a perfect, divine reality. This philosophical concept, commonly referred to as the theory of Forms, was explained by Plato in an excerpt from his *Republic* dubbed the "Allegory of the Cave." Plato's theory was that the truth is found in the "world of Forms," which exists beyond the physical reality that we humans perceive with our five senses.

In his "Allegory of the Cave," Plato asks that we imagine a group of people who have spent their entire lives trapped within a cave, forced to face a wall upon which shadows and reflections are projected by a fire that burns behind them. This reflection is a metaphor for the visual stimuli of our physical existence, the world of Forms. These shadows are not reality, though the people within the cave believe them to be real. Plato goes on to explain that philosophers are those few souls who began their lives trapped within the cave like everyone else. However, the philosopher comes to realize that he is, in fact, in a cave and is therefore able to find freedom from it. The philosopher then leaves the cave and comes to understand the truth of the world of Forms. From here, it is the philosopher's existential duty to return to the cave and help others liberate themselves from it. Of course, there will be some who do not wish to be freed. There are some people, in fact, who are so afraid of leaving the cave that they will kill the philosophers who try to shatter its illusions.

Just as the relationship between Sam and Dean existed as the worldly reflection of the conflict between Michael and Lucifer, there is yet another element where this "as it is in Heaven, so must it be on Earth" idea also applies—the archetypal relationships between fathers and sons, in reality as well as in mythology.

FATHERS, GODS, AND OTHER DADDY ISSUES

Look at you! Boo-hoo! Daddy was mean to me, so I'm gonna smash up all his toys . . . Play the victim all you want. But you and me? We know the truth. Dad loved you best; more than Michael, more than me. Then he brought home the new baby and you couldn't handle it. So all of this is just a great big temper tantrum. Time to grow up.

—GABRIEL, "HAMMER OF THE GODS" (5-19)

When it comes to the relationship between humans and God across many religious traditions, perhaps no other worldly relationship is used in comparison more than that of father–son/child. Many of the same feelings and difficulties exist between children and fathers as exist between humans and God.

The relationship between John Winchester and his sons, Sam and Dean, bears a number of similarities to the relationship between God and his angelic sons, Lucifer and Michael. In fact, even biblical lore uses a story about a father-son relationship as a metaphor for how humans are perceived by God. This biblical story is often referred to as the tale of the prodigal son and can be found in the Gospel according to Luke 15:11–32.

Basically, the story tells of a man who has two sons. The younger son (one might call him the Sam of the story) asked for his half of his inheritance, and so the father divided up the inheritance equally between his two sons. The older son used the money wisely and prospered. The younger brother, however, gathered up his inheritance and his belongings and journeyed to the city. There, he spent his money frivolously and hosted parties day and night. Needless to say, the younger son soon found himself penniless and friendless. He had no choice but to hire himself out as a pig handler, which in the Jewish world was the most loathsome profession one could have. All the son was allowed to eat was the same scraps that the pigs ate.

After a while, the son realized that even his father's servants were treated better than he was. He decided to return to his father and beg to be allowed to work as a servant in his home. The son even prepared a speech, planning to fall to his knees and humbly proclaim, "Father, I have sinned against Heaven before you! I am no longer worthy to be called your son! Please treat me as one of your hired servants." When the son was still a long ways off from his destination, however, his father saw him and came running to his long lost son. The son made his speech with sincerity, and his father's reaction was as follows:

> But the father said to his servants, "Bring quickly the best robe, and put it on him, and put a ring on his finger, and shoes on his

feet. And bring the fattened calf and kill it, and let us feast and celebrate! For this my son was dead, and is alive again; he was lost, and now is found." And there was a great celebration in the home.

—LUKE 15:22–24

The older brother (the Dean of this story) was out in the fields working when all this happened. As he got close to home that evening, he heard music and celebrating. Wondering what had happened, he asked one of the servants what was going on. When he learned that his good-for-nothing, irresponsible little brother had returned home in rags, the older brother fumed with anger. He was so mad, in fact, that he wouldn't even go inside the house. The father, hearing of this, went outside to see his older son. Their conversation went like this:

He answered his father, "Look! All these many years I have served you, and never once have I disobeyed your orders [Sounds a lot like Dean, doesn't it?]. *Yet you never gave me even a young goat so that I might celebrate with my friends. But when this son of yours who has squandered your property with prostitutes returns home, you kill the fattened calf for him!"*

"My son," the father replied, "you have always been with me, and all that I have is yours. But we had to celebrate and be glad, because this brother of yours was dead and is alive again; he was lost and is found."

—LUKE 15:29–32

Mythology is full of similar stories, in which a father must negotiate handling two very different sons. More often than not, the seemingly less deserving son receives the most attention. However, this is often because this son needs the most looking after ("Look after Sammy," said John Winchester to his older son). The most obedient and able son, of course, feels neglected even though the parent does not intend for this to be so.

LAZARUS RISING: THE MYTHOLOGY OF RESURRECTION

CASTIEL: I'm the one who gripped you tight and raised you from perdition.
DEAN: Why'd you do it?
CASTIEL: Because God commanded it. Because we have work for you.
    —CASTIEL AND DEAN WINCHESTER, "LAZARUS RISING" (4-1)

The concept of resurrection, more specifically of people being brought back from the dead, is found throughout religious mythology. Earlier, you read about the twice-reanimated Osiris, but perhaps no other story of resurrection is better known in the Western tradition than that of Lazarus. In fact, the *Supernatural* episode in which Dean is pulled from Hell and brought back to life is entitled "Lazarus Rising."

The story of Lazarus is found in chapter 11 of the Gospel according to John. It tells of a situation in which a man named Lazarus of Bethany, who was a beloved friend of Jesus and the brother of Mary Magdalene, fell ill. News of his illness was sent to Jesus, who did not express any concern and remained where he was for another two days. After these two days, he told his disciples it was time to go see Lazarus and, in John 11:14–15, said to them in a normal tone, "Lazarus is dead, and for your sake I am glad I was not there, so that you may believe. Let us go to him." A disciple named Thomas misunderstood what Jesus was saying and thought he meant that it was time to go to their deaths. And yet, he said to the others, "Let us also go, that we may die with him."

When Jesus arrived in Bethany, he found the family of Lazarus grieving his death. Martha, sister of Mary and Lazarus, lamented at how if only Jesus had been there Lazarus could have been saved. Jesus simply replies, "Your brother will rise again" (John 11:23). Martha believes Jesus is referring to the resurrection of the Final Judgment, but Jesus explains that he is going to raise Lazarus from the dead.

Jesus called for Mary and asked that he be taken to the tomb of Lazarus. He commanded those present to remove the stone that sealed the tomb. At first they hesitated, knowing that the decomposing body must by now have begun to smell. But Jesus told them to have faith, and they removed the stone. With the stone removed, Jesus simply called into the tomb, "Lazarus! Come out!" Seconds later, Lazarus emerged from the mouth of the tomb wrapped in his burial linens. Jesus told the others to take off his burial linens and put him in his clothes. This act of resurrection further encouraged people to follow Jesus, and ultimately this led his opponents among the Pharisees to begin plotting his death.

BOBBY SINGER:
MODERN-DAY MERLIN

Sam, Dean, I love you like my own. I do. But sometimes . . .
sometimes you two are the whiniest, most self-absorbed sons
of bitches I ever met. I'm selfish? Me? I do everything for
you. Everything! You need some lore scrounged up. You need
your asses pulled out of the fire. You need someone to bitch
to about each other. You call me and I come through. Every!
Damn! Time! And what do I get for it? Jack with a side of
squat!

—BOBBY SINGER, "WEEKEND AT BOBBY'S" (6-4)

In mythology, nearly every hero with an absentee father is blessed
with a mentor who acts in his stead. King Arthur had the counsel and tutelage of the wise sage Merlin. The Greek hero Jason
is taught by Chiron. In the myths of the Celts, the hero Cormac is
taught by Lugna, a friend of his late father, while in Vedic/Hindu
myths, the hero prince Arjuna (from the Mahabharata epic) is
taught by the god Indra. These figures are referred to in mythology as the "special teacher/mentor" archetype.

The archetype of the special teacher/mentor has a number of
common traits. The special teacher/mentor:

- Has some relationship or kinship with the hero's late or absent father. Merlin, for example, counseled Arthur's biological father, Uther Pendragon.

- Is of senior age, often portrayed as at least middle-aged for the time period in which the story was set (life expectancy differs from one age to the next).

- Possesses special knowledge, skills, equipment, and wisdom that the hero needs in order to succeed. Merlin educated Arthur in ethics, strategy, and politics; Indra gave magical weapons and combat training to Arjuna.

- Protects the hero from harm when he is defenseless, especially during infancy, and at times harshly scolds the hero for foolish or irresponsible behavior. Lugna hid and protected the child Cormac; Merlin often scolded Arthur for his poor judgment.

The archetype of the special teacher/mentor is most commonly seen in myths that deal with the "return of the lost heir/king" theme, in which the child of a murdered or usurped ruler returns to claim his birthright. Because the fathers of these exiled heroes and kings-to-be are usually absent, the presence of special teachers/mentors is necessary in order to validate their returns. After all, they would not be qualified to rule had they not received the proper training and education befitting a ruler. Basically, such special teacher/mentor figures allow the heir to return by schooling him in practices that are normally the responsibility of a father. For Sam and Dean Winchester, this figure is undoubtedly Bobby Singer.

Bobby Singer exhibits nearly all of the common traits of this archetypal figure:

- Despite once pulling a shotgun on the man, Bobby was a friend of John Winchester.

- Bobby Singer is middle-aged and is in fact much older than the hunters that are usually portrayed on the show.

- Bobby is a walking encyclopedia on all things supernatural, has an extensive library of rare texts, and is fluent in a number of languages (English, Latin, and Japanese, to name just a few).

- When their father is missing and they need help, the Winchester brothers go to Bobby Singer. Bobby's home also serves as a common sanctuary for the boys, as when Sam had to dry out from his addiction to demon blood. Bobby and Dean locked him in the "demon panic room."

The Winchesters need a mentor like Bobby, a man willing to stand beside them in the face of oblivion. Because, more than once, oblivion has been at hand and the Apocalypse nigh. Speaking of which, let's take a look at the Apocalypse.

≋ 11 ≋

ARMAGEDDON IT!

Honestly? I think the world's gonna end bloody. But that doesn't mean we shouldn't fight. We do have choices. I choose to go down swingin'.

—DEAN WINCHESTER, "JUS IN BELLO" (3-12)

In *Supernatural*, Sam and Dean are chosen to be the destined vessels of the archangel Michael and his evil counterpart, Lucifer. God's two most powerful creations plan to use the Winchester brothers as "meat suits" for a little "angel-on-fallen-angel" action. But the collateral damage from this final battle will wipe out millions of human lives.

In season 4 of *Supernatural*, the Winchester brothers have some rough times. When Dean allows Alastair to corrupt his soul and becomes a torturer in Hell, he unknowingly breaks the first of 66 Seals, which, similar to the Seven Seals of Revelation, will kick off the Apocalypse once they are all broken. The Winchester boys find themselves on the losing end of things, time and again, in their futile struggle to prevent Lilith and the other demons from breaking the remaining 66 Seals that will free Lucifer and kick off the Judeo-Christian End of Days. To make matters worse Sam kills Lilith, thinking this will stop the demonic queen from breaking the final seal . . . but instead finds out that the death of Lilith is the final seal. Unwittingly, Sam Winchester springs Lucifer from the pit.

As is often the case, things get worse before they get better. The Winchester boys later fail to stop Lucifer from unleashing the last of the Four Horsemen of the Apocalypse, and Death himself joins the terrible quartet. And when the Winchester boys cross paths with a young boy prophesied to bring future ruin upon the Earth as the Antichrist, the brothers choose to risk their own lives in order to help the boy escape from both the assassination attempts of Heaven's angels as well as the demonic influences of Hell's legions.

While the creators of *Supernatural* may have developed their own unique spin on the Judeo-Christian Apocalypse, they also relied heavily on certain traditional source materials related to the end of times.

THE APOCALYPTIC REVELATION OF SAINT JOHN

What I do have is a GED and a give 'em hell attitude. And I'll figure it out.

—DEAN WINCHESTER, "SYMPATHY FOR THE DEVIL" (5-1)

The apocalyptic revelation of Saint John is contained in the final book of the Christian New Testament and is more commonly known by the simple title of Revelation. However, it has gone by a variety of titles throughout history—Book of Revelation, Book of the Apocalypse, Book of the Revelation of Saint John, Apocalypse of Saint John, and [Book of] The Revelation of Saint John the Divine. Interestingly enough, of all the books in the Christian Bible, Revelation has had the most significant impact on the evolution of human history. For centuries, the decisions and policies of various monarchs and world leaders have been influenced by the apocalyptic prophecies written of in Revelation. It is interesting to note that in the modern vernacular the word *Apocalypse* has come to be used in reference to something akin to "a world-ending event." The original meaning of *Apocalypse*, however, was the same as that of its root word *apokalypisis*, a classical Greek term meaning "revelation."

In Revelation, the author identifies himself by the name of John. In religious circles, it is generally believed that the John who wrote Revelation, referred to as John of Patmos at the time, is the same John the Apostle who traveled with Jesus and wrote the Gospel according to John. However, many modern scholars challenge this assumption and believe that these "two Johns" were different individuals. Other commonly used names for the John who authored Revelation include Eagle of Patmos, John the Seer, John the Divine, and John the Theologian.

Patmos is the Greek island in the Aegean archipelago where John resided while writing Revelation. Most scholars agree that he was not on Patmos of his own free will but instead had been forced to live there as an exile. This belief stems from an interpretation of a short but significant passage that John wrote in Revelation 1:9, which explains that he was living "on the island, which is called

Patmos, for the word of God, and for the testimony of Jesus." Many have interpreted this to mean that John had been exiled to Patmos as punishment for trying to spread the teachings of Jesus.

John's exile, obviously, did not stop the continuing spread of Christian beliefs. It did, however, hinder John in supervising the growth of young churches. His Revelation text offers clues to this fact and actually begins as a series of letters to the Seven Churches of Asia, some praising and others criticizing their recent actions/ practices. At the time John wrote to them, the Seven Churches of Asia were among the strongest footholds for early Christianity. These churches were located in the Roman-Asian provinces of Ephesus, Laodicea, Pergamum, Philadelphia, Sardis, Smyrna, and Thyatira.

While certain events related to the End Times are mentioned in other parts of the Christian Bible, both Old Testament and New Testament, John's Revelation is the only biblical book that is entirely dedicated to the subject. Revelation is John's narration of what he claimed to be a divine vision in which an angel took him "in spirit" to Heaven and revealed the final events to him. In some places, these events are explained in literal terms. In others sections, they are portrayed through the use of symbols and metaphor. Unfortunately, John rarely explains which style of interpretation he intends. This unusual narration style has long made it difficult for religious scholars and clergy to agree on a standard interpretation. Just about every denomination of Christianity has its own unique take on at least one thing related to Revelation. When you think about it, however, this makes a strange sort of sense.

There are certain texts in the Judeo-Christian tradition in

which an individual will inquire about the exact dates and events of the End Times. However, the answer they usually get is that the Apocalypse, like death, will sneak up as a "thief in the night." No one is allowed to know until it happens. So perhaps Revelation was intentionally designed so that it would not be widely understood in advance.

66 SEALS VERSUS SEVEN SEALS

This demon, Lilith, is trying to break the 66 Seals to free Lucifer from Hell. Lucifer . . . will bring the Apocalypse. So, smoke 'em if ya got 'em.

—ANNA MILTON, "I KNOW WHAT YOU DID LAST SUMMER" (4-9)

As with much of the lore in *Supernatural*, there is a lot of Internet chatter going on about the mythical origins of the 66 Seals portrayed on the show. The breaking of these seals, according to the show's lore, can be done by accomplishing any sixty-six out of about six hundred potential seals. And, once sixty-six of these seals are broken, it kick-starts the opening scenes of the Judeo-Christian Apocalypse. Unfortunately, a lot of dishonest or just misguided people (mostly those scary creatures often referred to as "Internet Trolls") have posted a plethora of misinformation on the Internet—especially in wikis and forums—about this topic, often claiming that these seals can be found in some obscure or ancient text, usually one that has not yet been translated into English (or any other modern language, for that matter). After all, it's tough to check a source if you don't know how to read it. However, no valid texts of this kind actually exist.

While the creators and writers of the show did not allow viewers to witness the breaking of all 66 Seals, they did manage to write some details about several of these 66 Seals into a number of episodes:

1. Though viewers don't directly see it, the show explains that Dean Winchester broke the first seal when he was corrupted by Alastair and tortured souls in Hell.

2. In "Are You There, God? It's Me, Dean Winchester" (4-2) the spirits of the dead are resurrected in an event called the Rising of the Witnesses, which breaks another seal.

3. The resurrection of Samhain, which the brothers fail to prevent in "It's the Great Pumpkin, Sam Winchester" (4-7), breaks yet another seal.

4. The archangel Uriel breaks a seal by killing his brother and sister angels.

5. Rufus Turner identifies the causes of three more broken seals in "When the Levee Breaks" (4-21): (a) the extinction of ten species in the area of Key West, Florida; (b) the sudden blindness of an entire fifteen-man fishing crew in Alaska; and (c) the murder of sixty-six schoolchildren in New York by their own (probably demon-possessed) teacher.

6. The Winchester boys actually succeed in stopping Alastair from breaking another seal when the demon attempts to

kill two Reapers during a solstice. Alastair manages to kill one Reaper but not the second.

7. And, of course, the killing of Lilith was the final seal to be broken—by none other than Sam Winchester.

While they make for a very interesting plot element in *Supernatural*, the truth is that there are no 66 Seals in the Judeo-Christian mythos (or in any other related mythos, for that matter). *Supernatural*'s use of the number 66 for these seals more than likely has a pretty simple explanation. The demons have to break sixty-six out of six hundred seals, right? And 66 + 600 = 666, which most people know as the "number of the Beast" mentioned in Revelation.

However, the number 66 has a number of religious significances. So, just to be thorough, here are some facts related to the religious implications of the number 66:

- In the year 66 CE, Halley's Comet was visible from Earth (and, as we all know, Samuel Colt created his special pistol during a time when Halley's Comet was overhead).

- A rebellion of Hebrew tribes against the Roman Empire also began in 66 CE.

- There is a total of sixty-six books in the canonical Christian Bible (Old Testament plus New Testament).

- In the Islamic tradition, the numerological value of the name of Allah is 66.

- There are sixty-six verses in Lamentations 3 in the Old Testament, which is a wailing of suffering, hope, and divine revenge (sounds somewhat fitting to *Supernatural*, doesn't it?).

- There are sixty-six chapters in the book of Isaiah, the Old Testament prophet credited with foretelling the circumstances of Christ's birth as well as prophesying certain apocalyptic events.

While there may be no 66 Seals in the Judeo-Christian tradition, there are Seven Seals of the Apocalypse that are described in John's Revelation. According to the text, there is a book closed by Seven Seals. This book is opened by the "Lion of the Tribe of Judah," which is an alternative title for Jesus Christ. These Seven Seals, according to Revelation 5:6, are then broken by "a Lamb" with "seven horn and seven eyes, which are the seven spirits of God sent forth upon the Earth." The identities of these spirits are generally thought to be the seven archangels (see chapter 4).

With the opening of each seal, certain apocalyptic events are allowed to occur. For example, the breaking of the first four seals will unleash upon the Earth the Four Horsemen of the Apocalypse, who will be discussed in further detail later in this chapter.

The horrors that are unleashed by the Seven Seals (as set down in Revelation, beginning in chapter 6 and ending at the start of chapter 8) can be summed up as follows:

Seal 1—The White Horseman (The Conqueror, or a symbol of Conquest; however, there are differing interpretations of what this means)

Seal 2—The Red Horseman (War)

Seal 3—The Black Horseman (Famine)

Seal 4—The Pale Horseman (Death)

Seal 5—The "Vision of the Martyrs," in which John sees the souls of those who have been killed "for the Word of God" asking when they shall be avenged.

Seal 6—Begins with a terrible earthquake; the sun turns black, the moon turns red, stars fall out of the sky, and the planet's geography is violently changed; humans hide in caves, fearing God's wrath; lastly, 144,000 people from the tribes of Israel are granted protection from the terrible events still to come in the form of seals on their foreheads.

Seal 7—Marked by one half hour of silence in Heaven; then the "seven angels" will appear in order to sound the "seven trumpets" that mark the events related to the rise and fall of the Antichrist (more on this later).

THE FOUR HORSEMEN

Apocalypse . . . as in 'Apocalypse' Apocalypse? The Four Horsemen, pestilence, five-dollar-a-gallon-gas-Apocalypse?
—DEAN WINCHESTER, "ARE YOU THERE, GOD?
IT'S ME, DEAN WINCHESTER" (4-2)

Of all the figures associated with Saint John's apocalyptic vision, perhaps none have become more iconic of the End Times than the infamous Four Horsemen. They are, in a sense, the "generals" of the Apocalypse. Set loose upon the Earth with the opening of the first four seals, their arrivals will open the way for some of the most terrible events of Armageddon.

THE WHITE HORSEMAN: THE CONQUEROR

The first White Horseman is often referred to as the Conqueror, and there is some controversy regarding the meaning of his presence. According to the writings of Saint John, his vision of the White Horseman was as follows:

> *I watched as the Lamb opened the first of the Seven Seals. Then I heard one of the seven living creatures say with a voice like thunder, "Come and bear witness." I looked, and behold I saw a white horse! The rider held a bow, and was given a crown, and he rode out as a conqueror bent on conquest.*
>
> —REVELATION 6:1–2

There are some religious leaders and scholars who assert that this White Horseman is in fact a symbol of Jesus Christ, or is literally himself the Christ, returning to Earth in order to "conquer" evil. On the other hand, some of those who disagree with this view often point out that Christ's return is specifically mentioned in later verses of Revelation. This would seem to make the association of the White Horseman to Christ unnecessarily redundant.

Another theory that contradicts the "Christ as Horseman"

claim asserts that this Horseman is a symbol of the Antichrist, who is prophesied to conquer the world politically, financially, and militarily. This concept stems from the belief that the Antichrist, with his demonic powers of seduction and deception, will first unite the world under a single government (often referred to as the New World Order) and false religion. He will then lead a violent and worldwide persecution of those who refuse to follow his religion and rule.

Still others have interpreted the bow, crown, and conquest symbols to mean that the number of nations will decrease as wars of conquest are waged against smaller lands by the more powerful countries of the world. Many proponents of this idea believe that the White Horseman has already arrived, seeing as how such events have already occurred in recent periods of human history. Many view this rider as a symbol of international power politics in the form of military conquest.

Perhaps the various interpretations of the White Horseman explain why the creators of *Supernatural* chose to portray him as Pestilence. They likely chose to interpret the mention of "conquest" as a reference to the behavior of a virus. After all, viral organisms infect and take over healthy cells and use them to spread throughout the body; one might say that viruses are the "conquerors" of microorganisms.

THE RED HORSEMAN: WAR

While there is some debate as to the meaning of the initial White Horseman of the Apocalypse, there is next to none when it comes to interpreting the meaning of his brother the Red Horseman. It is almost universally accepted that he is a manifestation of War. According to the writings of Saint John, his vision of the Red Horseman occurred as follows:

When the Lamb opened the Second Seal, the second living creature said, "Come and bear witness." And behold another horse came out, this one fiery red. The rider was given the power to remove peace from the face of the earth, and to make men kill and wage war upon each other. To the rider was given a mighty sword.

—REVELATION 6:3–4

The Red Horseman will have the power to plunge the entire globe into a period of all-out war. The only real controversy related to the Red Horseman has to do with whether or not he has already arrived. Some claim that the mid-twentieth century to the present has been the age of the Red Horseman, pointing to such occurrences as the invention of the atomic bomb and other nuclear weapons as well as the increasingly global nature of warfare. There are some, such as members of the various apocalyptic-centered Protestant denominations of Christianity, who believe that the Red Horseman's "mighty sword" represents a nuclear weapon itself, the use of which would spell the end of the entire planet as well as every living thing on it. If any country on the planet launches a nuclear weapon, its enemies will launch theirs, beginning a domino effect that could mean multiple countries launching their nuclear arsenals. This is a sobering fact, considering that there are enough nuclear weapons currently in existence to turn this planet to dust several times over, even after years of downsizing and disarmament of the world's nuclear arsenals (during the latter years of the cold war, there were enough nuclear weapons to obliterate the planet over a hundred times).

Others believe that the nuclear association of the Red Horseman is wrong, since he is listed before the Black Horseman of Famine in John's visions. After all, how can there be a famine if the entire planet has been destroyed? However, those who follow this rationale fail to realize that nowhere in Revelation does it say that the events caused by the Four Horsemen will occur in the order that they were revealed to Saint John. When reading, most people tend to assume that events mentioned in a certain order are going to occur in a corresponding chronological order. When it comes to the occurrences of prophecies, however, such chronology often does not apply. For example, it is not made clear in Revelation if there will even be a pause or period of time between the release of the Four Horsemen. For all we know, they could all four come at once.

Even the creators/writers of *Supernatural* seem to have acknowledged this issue of chronology. For example, even though War is mentioned second in Saint John's Revelation, he is the first of the Four Horsemen to arrive on the show. The Winchesters tangle with War in "Good God, Y'all" (5-2). They succeed in bringing this Horseman down by chopping off his finger, thus separating him from his red-jeweled ring, the source of his powers (in *Supernatural* lore, anyway). I guess that's one way to get a ring off.

THE BLACK HORSEMAN: FAMINE

The prophecy of the Black Horseman, who is released by the breaking of the third seal, has received some close attention in recent years. Here is how Saint John described his vision of the Black Horseman:

> *When the Lamb opened the Third Seal, I heard the third living creature say, "Come and bear witness!" I looked, and behold I saw a black horse! The rider was holding a pair of scales in his hand. Then I heard a voice that seemed to come from among the four living creatures, declaring, "A quart of wheat for a day's wages, and three quarts of barley for a day's wages, and do not damage the oil and the wine!"*
>
> —REVELATION 6:5–6

Supernatural portrays the Black Horseman as the agent of a spiritual famine, causing people to become consumed by their desire for their vices. For example, in "My Bloody Valentine" (5-14), a man who had his stomach surgically reduced in order to lose weight eats so many Twinkies that he busts the staples and ruptures his stomach. A coroner who is a recovering alcoholic goes home and drinks himself to death. Even the angel Castiel, or at least his human vessel, is overcome by his desire for red meat and starts downing White Castle burgers by the mouthful. When asked by Dean how many burgers Castiel has eaten, the angel replies, "Lost count. It's in the low hundreds."

More commonly accepted interpretations of the Famine Horseman in Revelation, however, are usually more literal in nature. One interesting thing about the Famine/Black Horseman is that he doesn't exactly represent so much a shortage of food as an increase in its cost. You might say that this Horseman is a manifestation of financial hardship or global inflation. This interpretation is supported by the final line of the vision, where one of the four creatures declares, "A quart of wheat . . . and three quarts of barley for a day's wages, and do not damage the oil and the wine!"

In the time the text was written, a "day's wages" usually referred to a Roman silver coin, a denarius (plural form: denarii), which was considered a ridiculous price for only a quart of wheat or three quarts of barley. A single denarius commonly bought eight times as much of either. To put it into perspective, a quart of wheat was only enough for about one good meal and three quarts of barley enough to make three somewhat meager meals. As for the mention of "oil and wine," these were considered luxury items that were usually bought with whatever funds were left over after one's food had been purchased. However, if food cost all of one's wages, there would be nothing left to buy the luxury items such as the oil used to flavor and soften the bread, and wine to drink.

Just like the previous two Horsemen, there are some religious scholars who believe that the Black Horseman has already arrived. Proponents of this idea support their claims by pointing to recent events such as the collapse of the real estate and credit markets, the U.S. financial recession, and various global economic crises.

THE PALE HORSEMAN: DEATH

As with the Red Horseman, there is little debate as to the meaning of the fourth and final Pale Horseman—Death. Saint John described his vision of the Pale Horseman as follows:

> *When the Lamb opened the fourth seal, I heard the fourth living creature say, "Come and bear witness." And behold I saw a pale horse! The rider was named Death, and Hell followed with him. Both horse and rider were given power over a fourth of the earth to kill by sword, famine and plague, and by the wild beasts of the earth.*
>
> —REVELATION 6:7–8

One of the most common misunderstandings related to the Pale Horseman is that *pale* refers to a shade of white. There have even been mistranslations of the Bible that made it seem as if the first and last Horsemen were both white. The word *pale* actually refers to the color of death and decay or the pallid skin of someone who is sick or dying. As it is used in Revelation, therefore, the word would be more accurately interpreted to mean a "pale green" or "yellowish green" color.

THE SEVEN "BAD NEWS" TRUMPETS

The Seven Seals and the Four Horsemen are only the beginning of the bad news when it comes to the Apocalypse. On the heels of the Seven Seals come the blasts of the Seven Trumpets that will announce some of the most terrible horrors that humankind could ever experience. The trumpets are blown by "the seven angels," which are believed to be the same seven who surround the throne of God, often ascribed as the seven archangels (see chapter 4). Each trumpet blast announces a more horrible event than the one before.

The First Trumpet: Destruction of Plant Life

The First Trumpet of the Apocalypse will devastate the vegetation of the planet. It is recorded by Saint John as follows:

> *And the seven angels prepared to sound the seven trumpets. The first angel sounded, and there was cast upon the Earth hail and fire mingled with blood: and one-third of the trees were burnt up, and all green grass was burnt up.*
>
> —REVELATION 8:6–7

The Second Trumpet: Destruction of the Marine Environment

The Second Trumpet of the Apocalypse will destroy the world's oceanic ecosystem and marine life. The event is recorded by Saint John as follows:

> *And the second angel sounded, and a great mountain of burning fire was cast into the sea: and one-third of the seas were*

turned to blood; And one-third of the living creatures in the seas
died; and one-third of the ships in the seas were destroyed.

—REVELATION 8:8–9

The Third Trumpet: Wormwood

The Third Trumpet of the Apocalypse will bring an event that affects the fresh waters of the planet, resulting from the collision of a huge comet called Wormwood. The event is recorded by Saint John as follows:

And the third angel sounded, and there fell a great star from
Heaven, burning like a lamp, and it fell upon one-third of
the rivers, and upon the fountains of waters; And the name of
this star is called Wormwood: and one-third of these waters
were poisoned by Wormwood; and many people died from these
waters, because they were poisoned.

—REVELATION 8:10–11

You might wish to note that the usage of the word *poisoned* in the above citation is also alternatively translated as "made bitter" in a number of traditional versions of the Christian Bible. However, bitterness in taste was often related to the presence of poisonous substances.

The Fourth Trumpet: Darkening of the Skies

The Fourth Trumpet will affect the celestial bodies, especially the light given off by the sun and reflected by the moon. This trumpet also announces that the worst is yet to come. Saint John records his vision as follows:

> *And the fourth angel sounded, and one-third of the sun was affected, and one-third of the moon, and one-third of the stars; so as one-third of them all was darkened, and the days were darkened by one-third, as were the nights. And behold I heard an angel flying through the midst of Heaven, crying out "Woe, woe, woe to the inhabitants of the Earth because of the trumpets of the three angels, which are yet to sound!"*
>
> —REVELATION 8:12–13

The Fifth Trumpet: Locusts from the Pit

The Fifth Trumpet announces the first apocalyptic event that humans will not be able to dismiss as having natural causes, as one can understand by reading John's following description of it:

> *And the fifth angel sounded, and I saw a star fall from Heaven to Earth: and to him was given the key of the bottomless pit. And he opened the pit; and out of the pit arose smoke . . . and the sun and the air were darkened by the smoke . . . And out of the smoke came locusts that spread upon the Earth: and unto them was given power . . . And it was commanded them that they should not hurt the grass or trees or any green thing; but only those who have not the seal of God upon their foreheads. And to them it was given that they should not kill . . . but instead inflict torment upon them for five months: and their torment was like that of a scorpion's sting. And in those*

days many will seek death and not find it; many shall desire death, and death shall flee from them. And the locusts' shapes were like horses prepared for battle; and their heads were gold crowns, and their faces were like those of men. And they had hair like that of women, and teeth like lions. And they had breastplates of iron; and the sound of their wings was as horses and chariots running into battle. And they had tails like scorpions . . . : and their power was to hurt men for five months. And they had a king over them, the angel of the bottomless pit, whose Hebrew name is Abaddon, but in Greek is called Apollyon.

—REVELATION 9:1–11

Some have interpreted the above passage to mean that no one on Earth will be able to die. This idea may have inspired *Supernatural*'s season 4, episode 15, "Death Takes a Holiday," in which humans are unable to die for a short period owing to the absence of Reapers. However, the passage specifically says that only those who are stung by these locustlike creatures will be unable to die for five months. Basically, anyone who has not yet repented will find themselves the targets of these creatures. Once stung, people will be plunged into a five-month-long period in which the only sensation they will feel is terrible pain, a pain from which there is no relief, not even death.

The king of these creatures is referred to as Abaddon (Hebrew) or Apollyon (Greek). In either language, the meaning remains fairly the same—Destroyer. This figure is often thought to be the angel of death. Though some have associated this figure with the Fourth Horseman, this interpretation is not widely accepted since all of the Four Horsemen are mentioned in the verses that follow for the Sixth Trumpet.

The Sixth Trumpet: Slayers of Humankind

When the Sixth Trumpet blows, many people may welcome it. This trumpet will set loose upon the Earth four terrible angels who will leave mountains of corpses in their wakes. John explains the event as follows:

> *And the sixth angel sounded, and I heard a voice . . . saying to the sixth angel, "Loose the four angels which are bound in the great river Euphrates." And the four angels were loosed, which were prepared for that exact hour, day, month, and year, to slay one-third of humankind.*
>
> —REVELATION 9:13–15

The "four angels" are in fact the Four Horsemen of the Apocalypse. This may seem odd, since the Horsemen have already been discussed. However, remember that chronological order often gets muddled in prophetic works unless it is specifically stated.

In the next passage of Saint John's Revelation, the Four Horsemen come together to lead a massive army the likes of which the world has never seen (and, more important, will be powerless to stop). This army will mean the end of millions of human lives. Saint John portrays this fearsome legion as follows:

> *And the armies of the horsemen numbered two-hundred-thousand-thousand* [200 million] *. . . And then I saw the horses*

*and those riding upon them, who had breastplates of fire, and
of jacinth, and brimstone: and the heads of their horses were as
the heads of lions; and from their mouths spewed fire and smoke
and brimstone. By these was one-third of humankind killed, by
the fire, by the smoke, and by the brimstone that came from
their mouths. Their tails were like serpents, and had the heads
of serpents, and with them inflicted pain. And those not yet
killed by these plagues still did not repent of the works of their
hands, that they should not worship devils or idols . . . : which
cannot see or hear or walk: they also did not repent of their
murders, sorceries, fornications, or thefts.*

—REVELATION 9:16–21

Needless to say, any who see this army coming would do well
to run away, as fast as their feet can carry them.

SUPERNATURAL FACTS

In the portrayals of the Four Horsemen in *Supernatural*,
the element of Revelation in which they collectively lead
their divine army is left out of the story line. Of course, this
inconsistency could be easily explained by the fact that Sam
and Dean Winchester took down all four of the Horsemen
before they could complete their tasks.

The Seventh Trumpet: An End to the Horror

The Seventh Trumpet announces the end of the terrors brought by the preceding trumpets and marks the start of a new reign of Heaven on Earth for the righteous (to be discussed further on in this chapter). Saint John describes this as follows:

> And the seventh angel sounded; and there were great voices in Heaven, saying, "The kingdoms of this world are become the kingdoms of our Lord, and of His Christ; and He shall reign for ever and ever." And the four and twenty elders sitting before God fell upon their faces and worshipped God, saying, "We give you thanks, Oh Lord God Almighty, who is, and was, and is yet to come; because only you have the power to reign. And the nations were angry, and your wrath is come, and the time of the dead, that they should be judged, and that you would give reward unto the prophets and saints, and those who fear thy name, both small and great; and that you should destroy those who destroy the Earth." And the Temple of God was opened in heaven, and therein was seen the Ark of his testament: and there was lightning, and voices, and thundering, and an earthquake, and great hail.
>
> —REVELATION 11:15–19

THE RISING OF THE WITNESSES

The so-called Rising of the Witnesses is portrayed on the *Supernatural* series in "Are You There, God? It's Me, Dean Winchester" (4-2). In this episode, those who have died as a result of someone else's actions (or inactions) come back as angry spirits to take vengeance upon the living who caused their deaths. This event may have been inspired by a passage from Saint John's Revelation. An event similar to what happens on the show (though, admittedly, with a number of differences) is described by Saint John as follows:

And I saw a great white throne, and him that sat on it, from whose face the earth and the heaven fled away; and there was found no place for them. And I saw the dead, small and great, stand before God; and the books were opened: and another book was opened, which is the book of life: and the dead were judged out of those things which were written in the books, according to their works. And the sea gave up the dead which were in it; and death and hell delivered up the dead which were in them: and they were judged every man according to their works. And death and hell were cast into the lake of fire. This is the second death. And whosoever was not found written in the book of life was cast into the lake of fire.

—REVELATION 20:11–15

WHAT ABOUT CROATOAN?

SAM: Roanoke was one of the first English colonies in America. Late 1500s?

DEAN: Yeah, yeah, I do remember that. The only thing they left behind was a single word carved in a tree. Croatoan.

SAM: Yeah. And I mean there are theories—Indian raid, disease—but nobody knows what really happened. They were all just gone. I mean, wiped out overnight.

—DEAN AND SAM WINCHESTER, "CROATOAN" (2-9)

SUPERNATURAL FACTS

Rivergrove, Oregon, is a very real town located in Clackamas and Washington counties. The name of the town was created by combining "Tualatin River," a river that marks the town's southern border, with "Lake Grove," the name of a larger community on the other side of Lake Oswego to the northeast. The small town in *Supernatural* is a pretty accurate portrayal of the real location. As of 2009, the town of Rivergrove had a population of only 348 people.

In *Supernatural*, the apocalyptic "end game" of the demonic legions is the spread of a "Croatoan" virus that infects humans with homicidal rage. This plan is first discovered by the Winchesters in "Croatoan" (2-9), when Sam's vision of Dean killing a young man leads them to the town of Rivergrove, Oregon. They arrive to find the town in the midst of mass demonic possessions. After they find the word CROATOAN carved into a telephone pole, Sam refers to the fact that a similar word was found carved on an abandoned outpost in Roanoke, Virginia, where the colonists disappeared. Believe it or not, the so-called Lost Colony of Roanoke is no myth. This was a real event in American history.

In the year 1585, well before the pilgrims set foot on the New World with their landing at Plymouth Rock, the very first English settlement had already been established in Roanoke (in what is now Virginia). Sir Walter Raleigh initially supervised the endeavor, once he was finally able to receive a permission patent from the queen of England to create the first New World settlement. Unfortunately, neither Raleigh nor those who followed him had any idea what awaited them.

Raleigh did not depart with the first groups of colonists that left England in 1584 but instead remained in England and left the transportation of the colonists in the hands of fellow nobleman Sir Richard Grenville. The initial group consisted purely of men and did an excellent job of making enemies of the native tribes—they executed a native chief by burning him alive. This proved to have been a bad decision, because by the spring of 1585 they were running dangerously low on supplies. Sir Grenville volunteered to set sail and return with a relief and resupply fleet (more than likely, however, he just wanted out of there).

Grenville passed his authority over the Roanoke colony to Ralph Lane, promising to return immediately with supplies (which, by the way, Grenville never did). Unfortunately, it would seem that Ralph Lane was lacking in leadership ability, and the colonists had few skills when it came to living off the land. Not long after Grenville bailed on Roanoke, the colonists became almost totally dependent on the local Native American tribes in order to obtain enough food to survive. Then the colonists managed to once again royally piss off the natives by treating them rudely. Finding themselves out of favor with the local tribes, the stranded colonists were soon in the midst of a full-blown famine.

Eventually, a nobleman named Sir Francis Drake arrived at the Roanoke colony in 1587. He had just finished wiping out a nearby Spanish colony. What Drake found, however, was a village of colonists that looked more like living skeletons. Most were near the point of starving to death. Drake loaded up his ship with as many of the worst-case survivors as he could and took them back to England. Among the colonists Drake took with him was Ralph Lane. For reasons unknown, perhaps to make room on the ship, Drake left behind fifteen of his own men to reinforce the remaining colonists that he'd left behind. What happened after that remains a total mystery.

Neither Drake's men nor any colonists left behind were ever seen or heard from again. The missing included fifteen of Drake's men, nineteen male colonists, seventeen women, and nine children. To this day, no one knows for sure what became of them. However, the colonists left at least one clue behind.

No one was even aware of the fact that the Roanoke colony had vanished until almost three years later when in 1590 the delayed supply ship promised by Sir Grenville roughly five years before finally arrived under the leadership of John White. The supply ship's crew found nothing but a ghost town. The only clue the ship's crew could find as to the fate of the colony was a single word, CROATOAN, carved into the wood of a post near the fortification's gate (conflicting accounts claim it was carved into a nearby tree).

Some have argued that Croatoan was a Native American name for a nearby island located near present-day Cape Hatteras, North Carolina, which was inhabited by several local tribes. These history scholars have speculated that the remaining colonists, in order to survive, chose to integrate themselves into the Native American tribes on the neighboring island. However, no additional evidence has ever been found that could conclusively prove this theory. To this day, the fate of the Lost Colony of Roanoke remains a complete mystery.

Supernatural offered its own explanation for the lost Roanoke colony. According to Sam, John Winchester wrote in his journal that he believed Croatoan was the name of a demon of disease or pestilence, "sometimes known as Dever, sometimes Resheph." Dever likely refers to an ancient Mesopotamian name for a destructive spirit (remember that the ancient Mesopotamians did not really have a word for "demon") or class of malevolent spirits associated with disease. Resheph is the name of a god from the ancient religion of the Canaanites, which was later demonized by the monotheistic YHVH tradition of Judaism. This is not just an idea in *Supernatural*; there are some in the paranormal community who speculate that Croatoan is the name of a demon that just so happened to resemble the Native American name for the nearby island.

A CHILD OF DOOM

This child is half-demon and half-human, but he's far more powerful than either. Other cultures call this hybrid Cambien or Kateko. You know him as the Antichrist.

—CASTIEL, "I BELIEVE THE CHILDREN ARE OUR FUTURE" (5-6)

Perhaps the most notable thing about *Supernatural*'s portrayal of the Antichrist is Castiel's use of *Cambien* and *Kateko*. Figuring out why he would use these words takes a bit of digging. The only related meaning of the word *Cambien* comes from the Spanish language and translates as "to change." This may have been used on the show in order to refer to the power of *Supernatural*'s demon-human hybrid to "change" physical reality at will.

Uncovering the meaning of *Kateko*, however, is a little more involved. The word *Kateko* comes from classical Greek and occurs in one of the oldest translations of the Christian Bible. Mentions of the Antichrist are not restricted to the book of Revelation. This figure is mentioned in Second Epistle of Paul to the Thessalonians (or 2 Thessalonians for short). This was a letter, supposedly written by Paul of Tarsus (more commonly known as Saint Paul the Apostle), to the newly established Christian communities in the city of Thessalonica. As with many religious texts, there is some debate as to the authenticity of this claim, but that's not really an issue we need to deal with in this book.

In this early Greek translation of 2 Thessalonians the word *Kateko*, roughly meaning something like "withheld," "restrained," or "not allowed," is used in reference to the Antichrist that is to come. This usage basically meant that the Antichrist and/or his abilities would remain "restrained" until the appointed time. Some have interpreted the usage of this word to mean that the Antichrist is Lucifer or Satan himself, who at the time of Paul was restrained in the prison of Hell.

The specific passage written by Paul of Tarsus is as follows (emphasis added):

> *Don't you remember that when I was with you I used to tell you these things? And now you know what is* holding him back *[Kateko], so that he may be revealed at the proper time. For the secret power of lawlessness is already at work; but the one who now holds it back will continue to do so till he is taken out of the way. And then the lawless one will be revealed, whom the Lord Jesus will overthrow with the breath of his mouth and destroy by the splendor of his coming. The coming of the lawless one will be in accordance with the work of Satan displayed in all kinds of counterfeit miracles, signs and wonders, and in every sort of evil that deceives those who are perishing. They perish because they refused to love the truth and so be saved.*
>
> —2 THESSALONIANS 2:5–10

Another mention regarding the Antichrist comes from the first book of John (or 1 John for short). This passage explains that there will be many antichrists, but that only the final Antichrist will become the Beast mentioned in Revelation. This seems contradictory to the idea that an antichrist must be the devil (after all, if God only had one son, it doesn't reason that Lucifer would have several). John discusses the existence of these antichrist figures as follows:

> *Dear children, this is our final hour; and as you have heard that the antichrist is coming, even now I tell you that many antichrists have already come. This is how we know it is the final hour.*
>
> —1 JOHN 2:18

LUCIFER'S CAGE AND THE GRAND MILLENNIUM

SAM: What if you guys lead the devil to the edge, and I jump in? It'd be just like when you turned the knife around on yourself. One action . . . just one leap.

BOBBY: Are you idjits trying to *KILL* me?

—SAM WINCHESTER AND BOBBY SINGER,
"THE DEVIL YOU KNOW" (5-20)

The idea that Lucifer is imprisoned comes from the book of Revelation.

> *And I saw an angel come down from heaven, having the key of the bottomless pit and a great chain in his hand. And he laid hold on the dragon, that serpent of old, which is the Devil, and the Great Adversary, and the angel bound him for a thousand years, and cast him into the bottomless pit, and sealed him up, and set a seal upon him, that he should deceive the nations*

no more, till the thousand years should be fulfilled: and after
that he must be loosed for a season.

. . . But the rest of the dead would not live again until these
thousand years were finished . . . They shall be priests of God
and of Christ, and shall reign with him a thousand years.

—REVELATION 20:1–6

Lucifer will not stay in his cage forever, though, and after a thousand years he will be released from his cage (presumably during the time of Armageddon). Paul explains this as follows (comments are provided in brackets):

After one thousand years are over, Satan will be set free from his
prison and will go out to deceive the nations at all four corners
of the Earth—Gog and Magog—to gather them for battle. And
their numbers will be like the sand on the seashore. They will
march across the breadth of the Earth and surround the camp
of God's people [presumably the Jews], the city he loves [some
interpret this to mean Jerusalem]. But fire will come down from
Heaven and devour them. And the devil, the great deceiver, will
be thrown into the lake of burning sulfur, where the beast and
his false prophet will be thrown before him. They will be tor-
mented for all time.

—REVELATION 20:7–10

After Lucifer (or, some would say, the generic agent of evil often referred to as the devil) is defeated, God will appear for the Final Judgment of humankind.

The Winchester boys and their comrades-in-arms succeeded

in tossing Lucifer's troublesome butt back into his cage, of course, and so have succeeded in placing a temporary hold on the Judeo-Christian Apocalypse. Prophecy states, however, that Lucifer's eternal imprisonment will only come during the final days of the Apocalypse. So, if the world does not end, neither does the devil. This, of course, would leave some questions to be asked: Just how long will Lucifer be kept in his cage this time around? And, of course, what does all of this mean for Sam Winchester? Only time will tell.

CONCLUSION

Chuck Shurley is right: endings *are* hard.

What does one say to wrap up a book about a show as incredible as *Supernatural*? After all, it's hard to neatly close up everything about *Supernatural* (not that this book even comes close to covering "everything" about the show) when the story of the Winchester brothers has not yet come to a conclusion. Season 5 left us with so many questions, and for every answer season 6 provides we are left with even more questions. As the show moves into its seventh season, the answered questions are likely to be replaced with a whole new set of mysteries.

I could talk about stuff like "brotherhood" and "loyalty," or I could end with some idealistic gibberish about how Sam and Dean may get knocked down, but they always get up again. After all, "wounds heal, chicks dig scars, but pride and honor are forever." So maybe this book should, like the site of the battle between Michael and Lucifer, "end where it all began." A wise man once said something along these lines: "No matter what you want to say, someone has probably already said it better." Perhaps it would be best to let someone else's words end the book for me.

Let us close with some insight from the great *Supernatural* prophet Chuck Shurley, author of what will one day come to be known as the "Winchester Gospel":

> So, what's it all add up to? It's hard to say. But me, I'd say this was a test . . . of Sam and Dean. And I think they did all right. Up against good, evil . . . angels, devils . . . destiny . . . and God himself, they made their own choice. They chose family. And, well, isn't that the whole point?
>
> No doubt. Endings are hard. But, then again, nothing ever really ends . . . does it?
>
> —CHUCK SHURLEY (AKA CARVER EDLUND), "SWAN SONG" (5-22)

Now . . . if only the writers of *Supernatural* would explain to us exactly why Chuck Shurley vanished into thin air, immediately after he finished the writing of all of this. Honestly, it's almost enough to drive a person nuts, trying to figure all of this out. As Dean Winchester might say, "Good luck with that, Chuckles."

Enjoy the rest of *Supernatural!*

BIBLIOGRAPHY

The author would like to acknowledge his consultation of the following works during his research for and writing of this book:

Anderson, Rasmus B., and Snorri Sturlson. *The Prose Edda: Norse Mythology.* Lawrence, Kansas: Digireads.com, 2010.

Brown, Nathan. *The Rape of Lilith: The Degradation of the Dark Mother.* Germany: VDM Verlag, 2009.

Brown, Ronald K. Editor. *The Book of Enoch.* San Antonio, Texas: Guadalupe Baptist Theological Seminary Press, 2000.

Campbell, Joseph. *The Hero with a Thousand Faces.* Princeton, New Jersey: Princeton University Press, 1973.

———. With Bill Moyers. *The Power of Myth.* New York: Anchor Books, 1991.

Davidson, Gustav. *A Dictionary of Angels.* New York: The Free Press, 1967.

Graves, Robert, and Raphael Patai. *Hebrew Myths: The Book of Genesis.* New York: Greenwich House, 1983.

Hurwitz, Sigmund. *Lilith, the First Eve: Historical and Psychological Aspects of the Dark Feminine.* Einsiedeln, Switzerland: Daimon Verlag, 1992.

Koltuv, Barbara Black. *The Book of Lilith*. Berwick, Maine: Nicolas-Hays Publishing, 1986.

Kramer, Samuel Noah. *Sumerian Mythology*. Philadelphia: Pennsylvania Paperback, 1972.

Krishna, Dharma. *Ramayana: India's Immortal Tale of Adventure, Love, and Wisdom*. India: Torchlight Publications, 2000.

Leach, Maria. Editor. *Funk & Wagnalls Standard Dictionary of Folklore, Mythology, and Legend*. Harper and Row, 1984.

Patai, Raphael. *The Hebrew Goddess*. Detroit, Michigan: Wayne State University Press, 1990.

———. *Gates to the Old City: A Book of Jewish Legends*. New York: Avon, 1980.

———. *On Jewish Folklore*. Detroit, Michigan: Wayne State University Press, 1983.

Smith, Evans Lansing. *The Hero Journey in Literature*. Lanham, Maryland: University Press of America, 1996.

Sproul, Barbara. *Primal Myths: Creation Myths from Around the World*. San Francisco: Harper and Row, 1979.

Wolkstein, Diana, and Samuel Noah Kramer. *Inanna: Queen of Heaven and Earth*. New York: Harper and Row, 1983.

The following Biblical translations were consulted and cited throughout this book:

King James Version (KJV)

New King James Version (NKJV)

New International Version (NIV)

New Century Version (NCV)

Catholic/Latin blessings and Rite of Exorcism were cited from the *Rituale Romanum: Pauli V Pontificis Maximi*, published by the Vatican on June 10, 1925.

INDEX

Index

Index

Index